THE
LIVERPOOL
STORY

A Pillar Box Red Publication

©2016. Published by Pillar Box Red Publishing Limited, under licence from Bauer Consumer Media Limited. Printed in China.

ISBN: 978-1-907823-72-5

HISTORY OF FOOTBALL

THE LIVERPOOL STORY

MARTIN JOHNSTON

Edited by James Bandy of MATCH

CONTENTS

18 APRIL 1964 - LIVERPOOL PLAYERS CELEBRATE IN THE DRESSING ROOM AFTER BEATING ARSENAL 5-0 TO WIN THE FIRST DIVISION CHAMPIONSHIP IN 1964. THE CUP WAS A REPLICA MADE ESPECIALLY FOR THE OCCASION BUT THE CHAMPAGNE WAS REAL.

INTRODUCTION

THE NAME OF LIVERPOOL IS ONE THAT IS KNOWN AND REVERED THROUGHOUT THE WORLD OF FOOTBALL.

From humble beginnings the team came to be known as the 'Mighty Reds' and in the later decades of the 20th century began to eclipse every other team in England.

This is the story of how the club quickly grew to be ***one of the best teams in the Football League*** and went on to dominate the game in Europe.

It is a story of many heroes and a few villains, of ecstatic triumphs and heart-wrenching tragedies. A story filled with some of the greatest players in the world and tales of some of the greatest games.

From the original ***'Team of all the Macs'*** to ***back-to-back title wins*** and ***early Anfield legends;*** to ***the Shankly era*** and ***Bob Paisley's incredible trophy haul.*** It's all here, including 'the greatest day' and 'the miracle of Istanbul'.

We also throw the spotlight on some of the things that have made The Reds so successful: the links with Scotland, the great goalkeepers, the infamous Boot Room and the 22 members of the official Hall of Fame.

This is the story of Liverpool Football Club.

25 MAY 2005 - STEVEN GERRARD CELEBRATES WINNING THE CHAMPIONS LEAGUE WITH TROPHY. LIVERPOOL V AC MILAN - UEFA CHAMPIONS LEAGUE FINAL - ATATURK OLYMPIC STADIUM – ISTANBUL.

THE EARLY YEARS

1880s TO 1950s

THE EARLY YEARS

June 3, 1892, Liverpool Football Club is founded

ANFIELD ROAD HAD BEEN ONE OF THE FIRST GROUNDS WHEN THE FOOTBALL LEAGUE WAS FOUNDED IN 1888 BUT THE ORIGINAL TENANTS WERE EVERTON FC.

The Blues played their first game there against Accrington and went on to win the League in 1891. However, in the background trouble was brewing. The president and owner of the club, John Houlding, was a Tory MP and Lord Mayor of Liverpool.

He'd built the ground in 1884 and when Everton moved in Houlding was charging them £100 a year rent. However by the 1889-90 season this had risen to £250 and the President had also proposed that the club become a PLC. Both issues met with opposition from Houlding's fellow directors and the Everton players.

The rest of those in control wanted a fixed low rent to secure the club's future but Houlding was more ambitious and favoured expansion.

The infamous break happened on March 12 1892. Some of the rebels were holding a meeting when Houlding unexpectedly arrived. George Mahon stood up to give Houlding the President's chair. King John of Everton's response was, "I'm here on trial, and a criminal never takes the chair".

He formed Liverpool F.C. with 18 to 19 of the original members on March 15, 1892 at his house in Anfield Road. By 1894 the club had adopted the city's colour of red, and six years later began wearing the Liverbird on their shirts.

Almost all of Everton's backroom staff and players had defected to their new home at Goodsion Park so Houlding had to build his new club from scratch.

They played their first game in September 1, 1892, a friendly against Rotherham which they won 7-1.

Liverpool's first competitive match was an 8-0 win over Higher Walton three days later.

Almost a year later to the day they played their first ever league match, debuting in Division Two. Middlesbrough Ironopolis were the hosts and Liverpool won 2-0 with goals from Joe McQue and Malcolm McVean.

They would go on to win the Second Division title by eight points and gain promotion to the promised land of the First Division in their very first season.

THE REST OF THE 1890s

After struggling in the First Division, Liverpool were relegated in 1895 following a 'test match' decider with Bury. However, they bounced straight back, winning Division Two in 1896 and scoring 106 goals.

By 1896-97 Tom Watson, the most successful manager in the country, had taken the reins and would take them to fifth, ninth and runner-up spots before guiding The Reds to their first title in 1901.

"They would go on to win the Second Division title by eight points and gain promotion to the promised land of the First Division in their very first season."

THE 1900s

Tom Watson's third season was 1899-1900 and a decidedly average one to start the decade with. Liverpool finished 10th, with 11 away defeats doing the most damage.

The season that unlocked the trophy cabinet for the first time was 1900-1901. *An unbeaten 12-game run won The Reds the title.*

In 1902 Liverpool mourned the death of founder John Houlding. The team he'd created were now one of the best in England.

Sam Raybould was Liverpool's best striker of the period, becoming the first Reds player to score 30 goals in a season, in 1902-03. Just as vital for the club were the defensive performances of Alex Raisbeck, who captained the club to both league titles.

The second title win came in 1906 and was an outstanding feat, as Liverpool had been relegated in 1904. They won the Championship in their first season back after winning the Second Division in 1905. Goalkeeper Sam Hardy was one of the key figures as the title was won by four points from Preston.

Liverpool finished the 1908-09 season in 16th, but with a semi-respectable total of 36 points. They finished the season before in eighth but had only managed 38 points.

THE 1910s

Liverpool began the decade of the First World War in good form, finishing runners-up to Aston Villa in 1909-10.

The season included an incredible game when they beat Newcastle 6-5 and successive 5-1 wins over Woolwich Arsenal and Chelsea. But there were also too many defeats and Villa won the title easily.

The Reds then began a horrible slide into mediocrity. They finished 13th, 17th, 11th, 16th and 14th in the years running up to the war. It was something of a relief for the club when professional football was suspended in 1915.

The period also saw a dark moment in that 1914-15 season, when four Liverpool players and three Manchester United players were banned for life for fixing a game.

Liverpool performed poorly in the FA Cup, going out to Everton, Fulham and Newcastle in early rounds before making their first ever final in 1914.

The final was played at Crystal Palace and the Liverpool line-up included all four players who would be banned a year later. Liverpool went down 1-0 to a goal from Bert Freeman.

Also in the line-up that day was the legendary Ephraim Longworth, a stalwart captain who played over 300 games for the club.

ELISHA SCOTT

Liverpool's greatest goalkeeper

REGARDED BY MANY AS LIVERPOOL'S GREATEST EVER KEEPER, ULSTERMAN ELISHA SCOTT NEARLY SIGNED FOR MERSEYSIDE RIVALS EVERTON.

His older brother Billy played for The Toffees and recommended Elisha when he was just 17. Everton thought him too young but Liverpool didn't and the rest is history.

Liverpool signed Scott from Linfield in 1912, but before the First World War he found it very difficult to dislodge incumbent keeper Ken Campbell and was even loaned to Crewe Alexandra for a short period. However, by 1920 Campbell was allowed to leave Anfield and for most of the next decade Scott was to be first choice for Liverpool.

Described as 'lithe and cat-like' he played a key part in Liverpool's back-to-back title wins, missing just three games in 1921-22 and none in 1922-23.

Tales of his rivalry with Everton's Dixie Dean became part of Merseyside football folklore. A famous legend tells of the two players meeting in the street and Dean tipping his hat in greeting, only for Scott to dive on the ground as if saving an imaginary header.

In all, he made 486 appearances for The Reds and is still Liverpool's longest-serving player. Scott also won a record 31 caps for Ireland.

He left Anfield in 1934 to play for, and later manage, Belfast Celtic, where he was in charge until the club folded in 1949. In 13 years at the helm, Scott took them to ten league titles and six Irish Cup wins.

"Described as 'lithe and cat-like' he played a key part in Liverpool's back-to-back title wins."

THE EARLY YEARS

LIVERPOOL FOOTBALL TEAM OF THE 1930-31 SEASON POSE FOR A GROUP PHOTOGRAPH. THEY ARE BACK ROW LEFT TO RIGHT: HODGSON, GARDNER, BRADSHAW, SCOTT THE TRAINER, MCDOUGALL, J. JACKSON AND MCPHERSON. FRONT ROW: EDMED, CYRIL DONE, MORRISON, SMITH, LUCAS AND HOPKIN. AUGUST 1930.

THE 1920s

In the 1920s, Liverpool cemented their reputation as one of the best teams in England. They only finished outside the top ten twice and two more titles were added to the trophy cabinet.

George Patterson managed the club through the war, but in December 1919 David Ashworth became Liverpool's fourth manager.

The Reds improved drastically and had Liverpool's first-ever England captain in Ephraim Longworth at the back and their greatest-ever keeper, Elisha Scott, between the sticks.

They claimed fourth spot in the First Division in 1920 and 1921 and then went on to win back-to-back titles.

Ashworth had taken the team to the top in just three seasons. Fred Hopkin, signed from Manchester United in 1921, was a key figure.

Liverpool won the First Division easily in 1923, so it was very surprising when Ashworth quit at the end of the season to re-join Oldham Athletic. He later explained that living 43 miles from Liverpool was difficult for his disabled family.

Mattie McQueen then took the reins and immediately wrote himself into history by giving Liverpool another Championship win.

The rest of the 1920s would be more downbeat, though there were two top-five finishes in 1925 and 1929.

THE 1930s

The 1930s saw the quietest time in Liverpool's history.

From 1931 they slumped in successive years from 9th, to 10th, to 14th and then to 17th in 1934. A minor revival in 1935 saw a 7th place finish but it was a false dawn as The Reds were pitched into relegation dogfights with their lowest ever league finishes, up to that point, of 19th and 18th.

In 1928 George Patterson had taken over from McQueen for his second spell. He retired in 1936 to become club secretary. George Kay then took over as manager and three of his signings went on to become Anfield legends: Billy Liddell, Bob Paisley and Albert Stubbins.

Although points were hard to come by for The Reds during this period, they still managed to score a lot of goals, thanks mainly to two of the best forwards ever to play for the club: Gordon Hodgson and Jack Balmer.

Hodgson's 36 goals in 1930-31 beat the previous Liverpool record of 31 in a season held by Sam Raybould.

Balmer's 98 goals included the feat of a hat-trick of hat-tricks in 1946. He also scored the fastest goal in Liverpool history, after just ten seconds of the 1938 derby match.

GEORGE KAY

Manager 1936-1951

BEFORE JOINING LIVERPOOL AS MANAGER, GEORGE KAY WAS BEST KNOWN AS A ROBUST CENTRE-HALF. *He was born in Manchester and played with distinction for Distillery in Northern Ireland before moving to West Ham United in 1919.*

Kay captained West Ham in the infamous, inaugural 'White Horse Final' at Wembley in 1923. In one of those strange quirks of fate that football often throws up, he had started his career at Bolton Wanderers, the winners that day.

He took over at Liverpool in 1936 after leaving Southampton, where he had had five years in charge. When his tenure at Anfield was interrupted after three seasons by World War Two, he worked tirelessly to keep putting out the best sides possible. ***One of the servicemen he drafted in was Bill Shankly, whom Kay greatly impressed.***

His greatest triumph was Liverpool's title win in 1947. In that season he gave debuts to Bob Paisley and Billy Liddell in the same game, a 7-4 win over Chelsea. Jack Blamer and Albert Stubbins scored 24 goals each to spearhead the charge for the title. Needing to win at Wolves on the last day, The Reds won 2-1 and secured their fifth Championship.

In 1950, Kay returned to Wembley for the first time since 1923, leading Liverpool out on to the famous turf as manager this time. But Kay was to be unlucky again as Liverpool's FA Cup hoodoo continued and they lost their second-ever cup final, this time 2-0 to Arsenal.

OCTOBER 1948 - LIVERPOOL F.C. PLAYERS WHO HAVE PLAYED IN THE FIRST TEAM. BACK ROW: (L-R) E. SPICER, RAY LAMBERT, LAURIE HUGHES, BILL SHEPHERD, CYRIL SIDLOW, BILL JONES, PHIL TAYLOR, BILL FAGAN, JEN BRIERLEY, ALBERT SHELLY (TRAINER). FRONT ROW: JIMMY PAYNE, W. WATKINSON, D. MCAVOY, GEORGE KAY (MANAGER), COUNCILLOR S. RONALD WILLIAMS (CHAIRMAN), JACK BALMER (CAPTAIN), C. DONE AND BOB PAISLEY.

THE EARLY YEARS

18 MARCH 1950 - LIVERPOOL FOOTBALL TEAM POSE FOR A GROUP PHOTOGRAPH BEFORE THE LEAGUE DIVISION MATCH AGAINST WOLVES AT ANFIELD. THEY ARE LEFT TO RIGHT BACK ROW: PHIL TAYLOR, BILL JONES, RAY LAMBERT, CYRIL SIDLOW, BOB PAISLEY AND EDDIE SPICER. FRONT ROW: JIMMY PAYNE, KEVIN BARON, ALBERT STUBBINS, WILLIE FAGAN, BILLY LIDDELL.

THE 1940s

Liverpool won the first post-war title in 1947 after a period of rebuilding led by manager George Kay. A key part of that rebuilding was the signing of Newcastle United's talented marksman Albert Stubbins.

Stubbins went on to score 24 league goals, exactly the same number as his strike partner Jack Balmer. Balmer took the headlines, though, with his incredible feat of three hat-tricks in three games.

It was an amazing season for The Reds in many ways. Two legends made their debuts in a 7-4 victory over Chelsea; Billy Liddell (who also scored twice) and Bob Paisley. The team that year also included Phil Taylor, who would go on to manage the club.

A nail-biting final day of the league campaign saw Liverpool win at Wolves to clinch the title, just one point ahead of rivals Manchester United.

Despite Liddell's wing wizardry and the goals of the Balmer/Stubbins partnership, Liverpool struggled in the other two seasons of the decade. They finished 11th in 1948, when Arsenal finished top, and 12th in 1949 as Portsmouth won the first of back–to–back titles.

THE 1950s

The next season saw the beginning of a slide into the Second Division and the worst decade in the club's history.

In 1950 Liverpool lost their second FA Cup final 2-0 to Arsenal, thanks mainly to The Gunners nullifying the threat of Billy Liddell. Liverpool's winger had terrorised their defence in two recent league games and they knew they had to stop him. Their plan worked, and two goals from Reg Lewis won them the Cup.

That season Liverpool finished eighth in Division One, the next season ninth and in 1952 the team slid to 11th. Despite increasingly poor results, the fans were still turning out. In February 1952 Liverpool recorded their highest home crowd when they beat Wolves 2-1 in front of 61,905 in the fourth round of the FA Cup.

Bob Paisley and Cyril Done scored the goals. Things were about to get a whole lot worse for those fans as The Reds slumped to 17th the following season, and then in 1954 finished at the bottom of a table for the first and only time in their history.

They then suffered their worst ever loss of 1-9 against Birmingham in December of the 1954-55 season. By 1959, after languishing in the second tier for four seasons, manager Phil Taylor resigned, ushering in the 'Shankly era'.

LIVERPOOL'S SECOND FA CUP FINAL, 1950

Reds lose out to Arsenal

IN 1950, LIVERPOOL TRAVELLED TO WEMBLEY FOR THE FIRST TIME EVER. IT WAS ALSO THEIR FIRST FA CUP FINAL FOR 36 YEARS. *This was still, and remained for quite a while afterwards, a competition The Reds struggled in.*

They had travelled in a confident mood to London by train. Their confidence was well-founded. After all, they had beaten their opponents Arsenal home and away in recent weeks and seen off city rivals Everton 2-0 in the semi-final at Maine Road. ***The Reds felt that after the disappointment of 1914, this was finally going to be their year.***

But it was to be another heart-breaking afternoon for The Reds as Arsenal, captained by future Manchester City manager Joe Mercer, set about negating Liverpool's main threat, Billy Liddell. Although predictably circumspect in the press afterwards, ***Liddell was on the end of some heavy tackles and his ability to influence the game was curtailed.***

The Arsenal side that day also included England cricketer Denis Compton, but it was goals from Reg Lewis in either half which enabled them to win the cup 2-0.

Bob Paisley suffered more than most Reds players as he was controversially left out of the side by manager George Kay and replaced by his best friend, Bill Jones. Although he was to make up for it with plenty of fantastic moments later in his career, the pain of this, his worst moment, apparently never left him.

ALBERT STUBBINS

Sgt. Pepper's Lonely Hearts Club striker

Although born in Wallsend, Geordie lad Albert Stubbins spent his early years in the United States.

When he made his goalscoring debut for Liverpool in 1946, he had already scored 232 goals in 190 games in wartime football, mainly for his home-town club Newcastle United.

His huge fee of £12,500 was a club record at the time for The Reds and a mark of how highly his talents were regarded at the end of the war.

An immensely popular figure at Anfield, Stubbins only missed two league games in 1946-47 as his 28 goals (24 in the league) helped The Reds win the first post-war title. He also scored 24 more the next season, including four against Huddersfield Town. He formed a devastating partnership over that time with Scouser Jack Balmer.

He played in Liverpool's FA Cup final defeat to Arsenal in 1950, but it was one of only 18 appearances that season. Later that year, however, he scored five goals as the Football League beat the Irish League 6-3 at Bloomfield Road, Blackpool.

The last of Stubbins' 178 games for Liverpool came at Stoke City in 1953. He finished with a goal tally of 83, an amazing record of almost a goal every other game.

He became a sports journalist after retiring from football and spent some time back in the USA. He also has the unusual distinction of being the only footballer pictured on the famous cover of The Beatles' *Sgt. Pepper's Lonely Hearts Club Band.*

BILLY LIDDELL

The one and only

William Beveridge 'Billy' Liddell, an unassuming, modest Scot, was in most people's eyes Liverpool's greatest ever player. Even the mention of his name can put a smile and a faraway look on the faces of Reds fans of a certain age.

Yet he would never have joined the club were it not for a tip-off from Manchester United legend (and fellow Liverpool player) Sir Matt Busby.

Liddell was a lightning-quick, two-footed winger who could also play at inside-centre. He was equally comfortable going to the by-line to beat a full-back or cutting inside to take his opponent on. He also had a pile-driver of a shot which accounted for many of his 228 goals for the club.

Signing in 1939 as the country went to war, 'King Billy' eventually made his debut in Liverpool's 1946-47 championship-winning season, scoring twice (including a goal direct from a corner) in a 7-4 win over Chelsea. His best return was in 1955-56 when he scored 33 goals. Liddell played 29 times for Scotland, scoring eight times, and was inducted into the Scottish Football Hall of Fame in 2008.

Nowadays we'd say that Billy Liddell was 'part of Liverpool's DNA', but back then they just re-named the team 'Liddellpool'. He played his last game in 1960 with 21 years and 534 games under his belt for the club he loved so much.

He went on to become a well-known figure in Liverpool civic life, serving as a Justice of the Peace and as bursar of Liverpool University.

THE 1960s

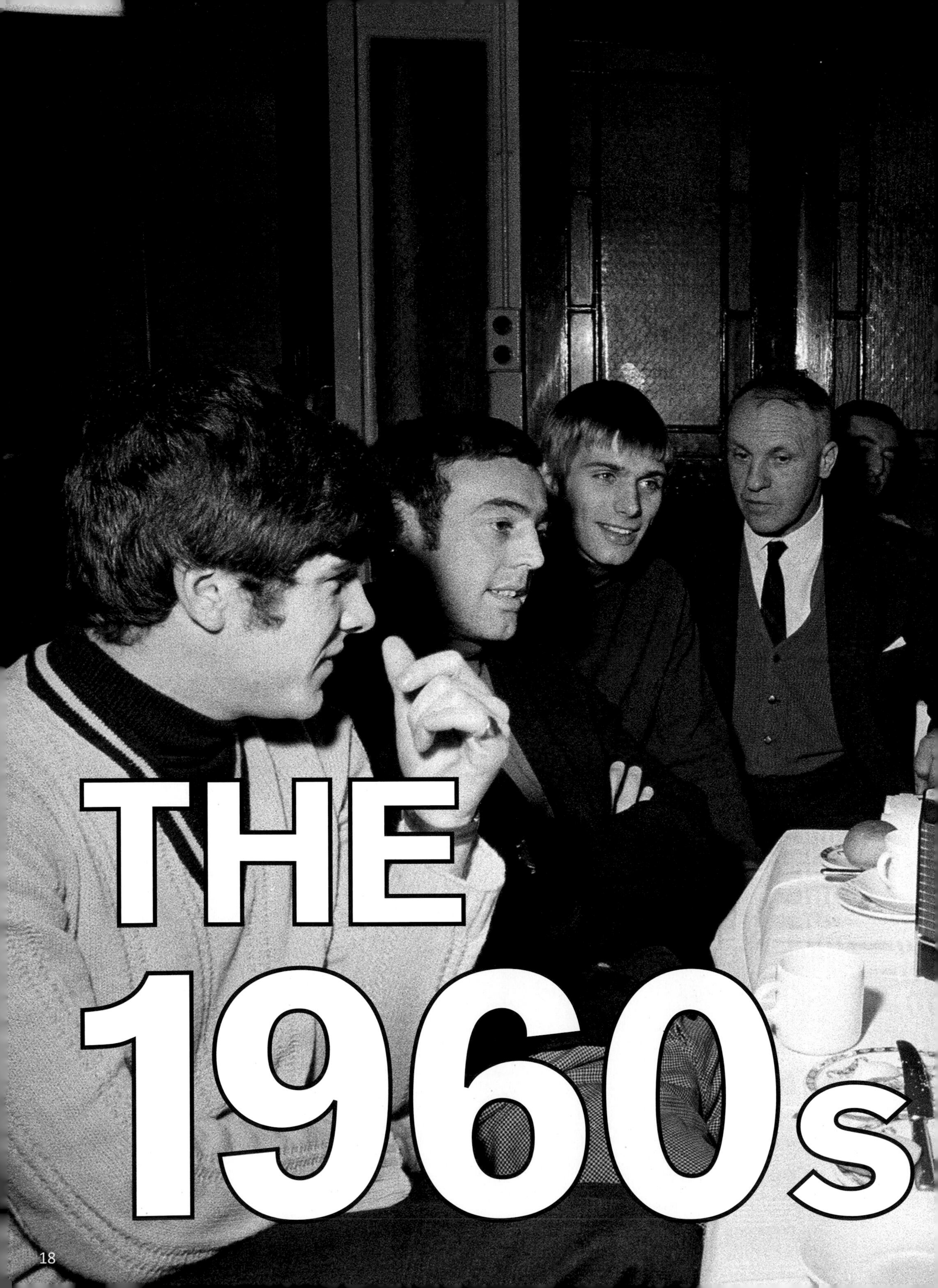

3 MARCH 1969 - LIVERPOOL MANAGER BILL SHANKLY LISTENING TO THE FA CUP DRAW WITH SOME OF HIS PLAYERS OVER LUNCH AT THEIR GROUND. THEY ARE ALUN EVANS, IAN ST. JOHN, EMLYN HUGHES, RON YEATS AND GEOFF STRONG.

IN THE 1960S LIVERPOOL SHOOK OFF THEIR TAG OF ALSO-RANS AND BECAME ONE OF THE MOST FEARED TEAMS IN ENGLAND. BY THE END OF THE NEXT DECADE THEY WOULD BE THE BEST IN THE COUNTRY AND WOULD TAKE THEIR PLACE AT THE TOP TABLE OF EUROPEAN FOOTBALL.

The Reds started the decade in Division Two and with two club legends making the headlines for different reasons.

Bill Shankly had taken over in December 1959, and the scale of his task became abundantly clear when Liverpool lost 0-4 to Cardiff City in his first game.

At the start of 1960-61 season, in August 1960, 'King' Billy Liddell played his last game. He'd played 534 times and was adored by the fans.

After taking a season to get the Red machine working his way and building a new team around his 'colossus', Ron Yeats, Shankly had his team back in the First Division in 1962. They won Division Two comfortably and were promoted with five games to spare.

Merseyside rivals Everton won the league in 1962-63 but Liverpool had battled to a creditable eighth, drawing twice in the derbies with the champions.

In 1964, however, the tables were turned as Shankly guided his team to their first title in 17 years. Everton were five points adrift in third, a point behind runners-up Manchester United.

1964 was also significant as the year Liverpool wore the all-Red strip for the first time.

Shankly believed it would give his team another edge, "red for danger, red for power", he explained.

SEASON	DIVISION	P	W	D	L	F	A	D	POS
1960-61	Division 2	42	21	10	11	87	58	52	3rd
1961-62	Division 2	42	27	8	7	99	43	62	1st
1962-63	Division 1	42	17	10	15	71	59	44	8th
1963-64	Division 1	42	26	5	11	92	45	57	1st
1964-65	Division 1	42	17	10	15	67	73	44	7th

THE TEAM TRAINING AT MELWOOD DRIVE, WEST DERBY. MANAGER BILL SHANKLY STARTS FIVE OF HIS TEAM OFF IN A 100 YARD SPRINT. LEFT TO RIGHT: WHITE, LEWIS, HUNT, MELIA AND A' COURT. 13 OCTOBER 1961.

Things could only get better and in 1965 Liverpool shook off their FA Cup hoodoo to win the trophy for the first time. They beat fierce rivals Leeds United 2-1 in extra-time.

It's probably fair to say that winning the Cup had more cachet back then and it was considered a massive achievement. It was no surprise, then, when Shankly said "that was the greatest day".

A sensational three years of dominance continued the next season as Liverpool won the 1965-66 First Division title by six points from Leeds and Burnley.

They also made it through to their first ever European final, losing 2-1 in extra-time of the Cup Winners' Cup to Borussia Dortmund.

Liverpool finished fifth in 1967, third in 1968 and were runners-up in 1969 as Leeds got some revenge for 1965 and 1966 by becoming champions.

SEASON	DIVISION	P	W	D	L	F	A	D	POS
1965-66	Division 1	42	26	9	7	79	34	61	1st
1966-67	Division 1	42	19	13	10	64	47	51	5th
1967-68	Division 1	42	22	11	9	71	40	55	3rd
1968-69	Division 1	42	25	11	6	63	24	61	2nd
1969-70	Division 1	42	20	11	11	65	42	51	5th

BILL SHANKLY

Two words that will forever be linked with Liverpool Football Club, whatever happens in the future, are: Bill and Shankly

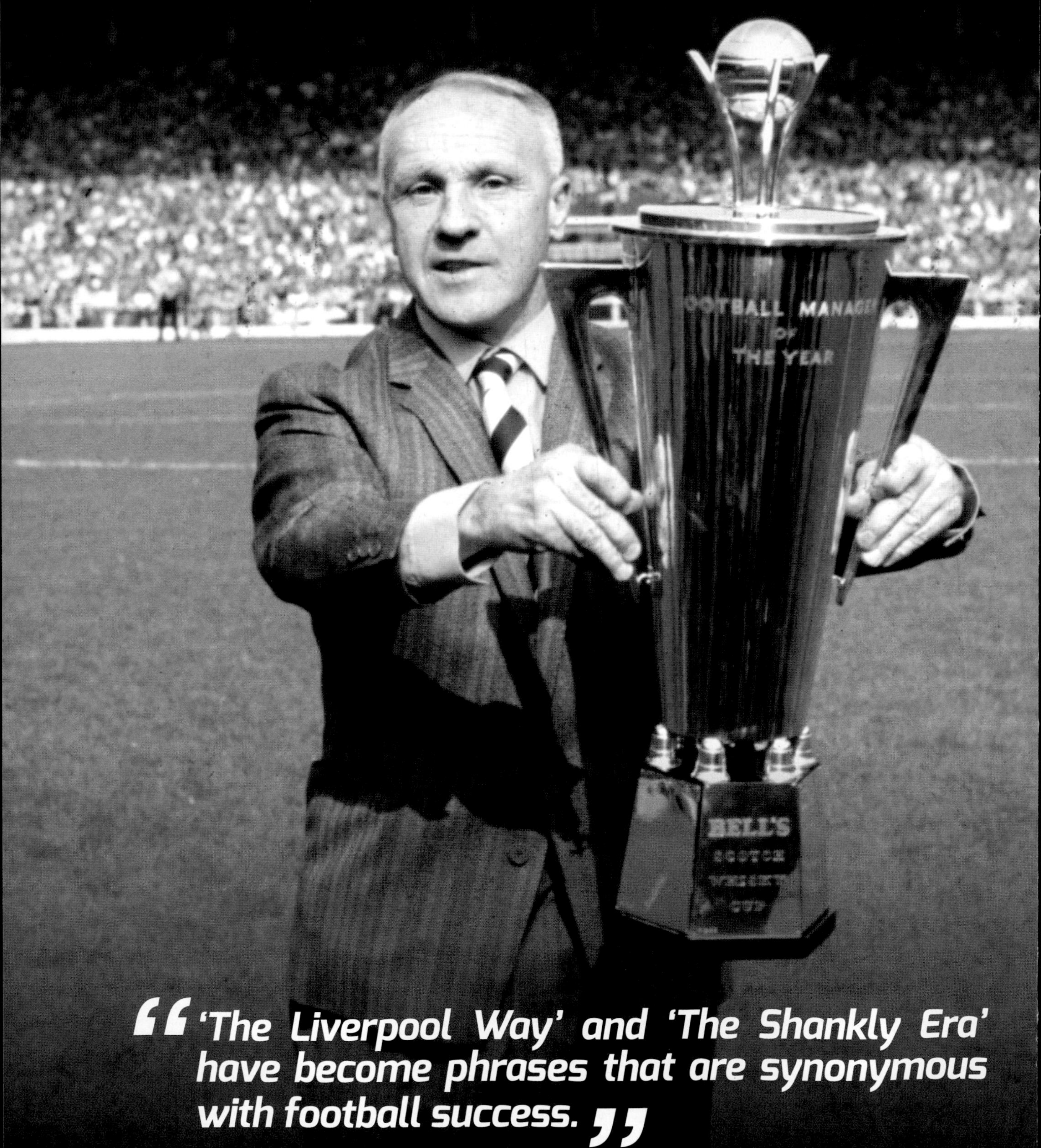

“‘The Liverpool Way’ and ‘The Shankly Era’ have become phrases that are synonymous with football success.”

ANOTHER SCOT WHO GAVE EVERYTHING HE HAD FOR A CLUB HE FELL IN LOVE WITH, *Shankly was charismatic and outspoken but conversely deferential and full of praise for opponents he respected.*

Other managers won more but he changed the club so much that 'The Liverpool Way' and 'The Shankly Era' have become phrases that are synonymous with football success.

Shankly led the Kop-inspired Reds to their first ever FA Cup triumph the following year and then won the First Division title again in 1966. In 1973 came Liverpool's first European trophy, the UEFA Cup, in the same season as their eighth Championship.

He retired in 1974 soon after he had led his team to a second stunning FA Cup final win over Newcastle. Through the infamous 'Boot Room' he left a legacy that would see the club become the best in Europe. He also left enough quotes to fill an entire bookshop.

Shankly saw the potential of a Second Division club in the doldrums and dragged it kicking and screaming to the top of the First Division. He arrived at Anfield from Huddersfield Town in 1959, having been interviewed and rejected eight years earlier.

By 1962 he had taken Liverpool back into the First Division and won the title in 1964. By then he had also created an aura around the club that the fans readily bought into. They flocked to Anfield and began to sing, chant and wear their colours like never before.

LIVERPOOL WIN THE FIRST DIVISION IN 1964

Liverpool are back where they belong

BILL SHANKLY'S FIRST MAJOR TROPHY WITH THE REDS CAME IN 1964, JUST ONE SEASON AFTER THEIR RETURN FROM THE SECOND DIVISION WHICH THEY WON AS CHAMPIONS IN 1962.

It was Liverpool's sixth title and came in some style, won with three games still to play and with goals galore. Shankly's side scored five goals or more on six occasions, crashing six past Wolves, Stoke, Sheffield United and Ipswich.

After the Ipswich game and a rare 0-1 defeat at Fulham, The Reds went on a seven-match winning run during which they conceded just two goals.

With wingers Ian Callaghan and Peter Thompson (both of whom played in every game) supplying the crosses and Roger Hunt (who only missed one game) the finishes, Liverpool scored 60 goals at home and 92 overall. They also kept 13 clean sheets as they finished four points ahead of Manchester United, with Everton in third.

According to Hunt, the secret of Liverpool's success was that "We were the fittest team in the country". *All due to Shankly's strict training regimes and the infamous Melwood 'Sweat Box'.*

The title was wrapped up in April with a 5-0 win over Arsenal at Anfield, where the turnstiles had to be closed an hour before kick-off because the ground was already full. Spare a thought for Arsenal keeper Jim Furnell, who had started the season at Anfield and even managed two appearances as understudy to Tommy Lawrence.

> "We were the finest team in the country."

ROGER HUNT

'Sir' Roger, the goal machine

"As well as scoring a lot of goals, Hunt specialised in scoring famous goals."

ROGER HUNT WAS THE ONLY LIVERPOOL PLAYER TO PLAY IN ENGLAND'S 1966 WORLD CUP FINAL WIN, *and to date no other Reds player has bettered his league record of 245 goals. No wonder the Kop dubbed him 'Sir' Roger.*

Hunt was signed from Stockton Heath (now known as Warrington Town), his local club in Cheshire. He scored on his debut as The Reds beat Scunthorpe 2-0 in 1959 and his goals were a key factor in Liverpool gaining promotion from Division Two in 1962. In all, he scored 41 goals in 41 games that season. Bill Shankly reportedly said "Christ, this one can play!" the first time he watched him.

He also played 41 of 42 games in 1963-64, scoring 31 goals, when Liverpool won the First Division for the sixth time and the first time under Shankly.

As well as scoring a lot of goals, Hunt specialised in scoring famous goals. He scored the first ever goal on Match of the Day in 1964 and the first goal in Liverpool's FA Cup final win over Leeds United in 1965.

Hunt also scored 18 times for England, including three during the 1966 World Cup, prompting captain Bobby Moore to say "Roger Hunt is a player's player. He is probably appreciated more by those who play with him and against him, than by those who watch him".

By the time he left to play for Bolton, 'Sir' Roger had scored 286 times for Liverpool in 404 games.

LIVERPOOL FINALLY WIN THE CUP IN 1965

The greatest day

IT TOOK 73 YEARS AND A PERIOD OF NERVY EXTRA-TIME FOR LIVERPOOL TO FINALLY WIN THE FA CUP Bill Shankly (who else?) finally ended the jinx, leading The Reds to a 2-1 win over Don Revie's Leeds United in 1965.

FA CUP FINAL AT WEMBLEY STADIUM. LIVERPOOL 2 LEEDS UNITED 1. MANAGERS ON THE BENCH, DON REVIE OF LEEDS AND BILL SHANKLY OF LIVERPOOL. 1 MAY 1965.

FA CUP FINAL AT WEMBLEY STADIUM - 1 MAY 1965. LIVERPOOL 2 V LEEDS UNITED 1. LIVERPOOL PLAYERS CELEBRATE ON THE PITCH AFTER THEIR WIN AS LEEDS PLAYERS WALK OFF DEJECTED.

LIVERPOOL NEEDED REPLAYS AGAINST STOCKPORT COUNTY AND LEICESTER CITY, BUT THEY HAD ONLY CONCEDED TWO GOALS ON THE WAY TO THE SEMI-FINAL AGAINST CHELSEA AT VILLA PARK. All season the players had felt the cup was theirs. A Willie Stevenson penalty was enough to book their passage to the final for only the third time.

The final itself was a tough game against a traditionally hard-nosed Leeds side, with few chances falling to either side. Ten minutes into the match the name Gerry Byrne entered Liverpool folklore. Breaking his collar bone after a collision with United's Bobby Collins, Byrne played on and supplied the cross for Roger Hunt to score the first goal.

Bob Paisley said of Byrne later: "He never got among the lads and was the quiet one in that cup-winning side. But he never shirked anything and was tough as they come, as he proved at Wembley."

Hunt's goal came three minutes into extra-time but Billy Bremner equalised soon after. With both sides out on their feet, on 111 minutes Ian Callaghan found an unmarked Ian St. John and his close-range header secured Liverpool's first ever FA Cup win.

After taking so long to get their hands on the cup, it is still hailed by many fans as the club's greatest day.

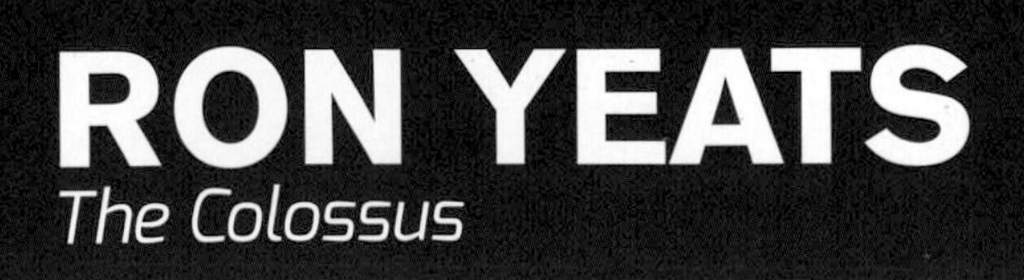

RON YEATS

The Colossus

> ***"Shankly called him 'a colossus'."***

RON YEATS WAS SUCH A CENTRAL FIGURE IN LIVERPOOL'S REBUILT 1960S TEAM THAT MANY OF BILL SHANKLY'S INFAMOUS QUOTES FROM THAT TIME ARE ABOUT HIM.

Shankly called him 'a colossus' and invited the press to walk around him and marvel at the new 'mountain' at the heart of his team. "With him in defence we could play Arthur Askey in goal", his manager said.

Shankly also used Yeats as his model for the new all-red kit that he decided to introduce in a game against Anderlecht in 1964. On seeing his captain decked out totally in red, his notion that that the team would look stronger was confirmed. "You look 7ft tall, son!" he said.

Like so many of Liverpool's greats, Yeats was a Scot, born in Aberdeen but signed from Dundee in 1961. His toughness and skill matched his 6ft 2in frame and he was a perfect skipper for Shankly's side.

He made his debut in 1961 in a 2-0 away win against Bristol Rovers, but it took two years to register his first goal, the only goal of the game against Manchester United at Old Trafford in 1963.

He led Liverpool to First Division titles in 1964 and 1966, with a trip up the Wembley steps to collect the FA Cup sandwiched in between in 1965.

'Big Ron' left to become player-manager of Tranmere in 1971, having played 454 games for The Reds. He also managed Barrow and had a short period in the USA with the Santa Barbara Condors. Strangely, he was largely ignored by Scotland and was capped only four times.

LIVERPOOL WIN THE FIRST DIVISION IN 1966

Shankly and Liverpool's third trophy in a row

THE NAME JOHN OGSTON WON'T MEAN MUCH TO LIVERPOOL FANS NOW, BUT HE WAS THE ONLY PLAYER TO SIGN FOR LIVERPOOL AHEAD OF THE TITLE-WINNING 1965-66 SEASON. A goalkeeper known as 'Tubby', he went on to make just one appearance.

CELTIC CAPTAIN BILLY MCNEILL, AND LIVERPOOL CAPTAIN RON YEATS, SHAKE HANDS BEFORE THE FIRST LEG OF THE EUROPEAN CUP WINNERS' CUP SEMI-FINAL AT CELTIC PARK, GLASGOW. 15 APRIL 1966.

THE SEASON STARTED WELL, PARTICULARLY FOR CENTRE-FORWARD ROGER HUNT, WHO WOULD END UP WITH A WORLD CUP WINNER'S MEDAL AND WHO SCORED TEN GOALS IN THE FIRST NINE GAMES, ENDING UP WITH 32 FOR THE SEASON.

Other highlights included a 5-0 demolition of Everton in the Merseyside derby at Anfield and a run of seven clean sheets for keeper Tommy Lawrence and his defence. The Reds also returned from a tough midweek game against Juventus in Turin to beat Aston Villa on the Saturday with two rare goals from winger Peter Thompson.

The traditional Christmas double fixture saw them share the spoils with Leeds United as they lost 0-1 at Anfield but won the next day 1-0 at Elland Road, with Gordon Milne scoring.

A 2-1 home win over Chelsea at the end of April, thanks to another Roger Hunt brace ensured Liverpool's seventh title, as they broke Leeds' hearts again, leaving them and Burnley trailing by six points.

Liverpool also got to their first ever European final in 1966, losing 2-1 to Borussia Dortmund at Hampden Park. As well as Juventus they also beat Standard Liege, Honved and Celtic on the way.

SPOTLIGHT ON: LIVERPOOL'S FAMOUS SCOTS

Liverpool – an English team made great by Scottish players

RON YEATS

THERE ARE CURRENTLY 22 PLAYERS WHO HAVE MADE THE LIVERPOOL FC OFFICIAL HALL OF FAME. *Amazingly, eight of them are Scots, which is even more astonishing when you realise that there are only six Scousers on that list.*

Starting a club from scratch, Liverpool owner John Houlding had to find players quickly and soon realised that Scotland was a source of immense talent.

The club's first ever captain was ***Scot Andrew Hannah,*** signed from the successful Renton club and part of a Liverpool team with so many Scottish players that they became known as 'The Team of all the Macs'.

Among those Macs was ***Matt McQueen,*** who was so versatile he played on the wing, in goal, became a qualified referee and managed Liverpool to the title in 1923. However, ***Alex Raisbeck*** from Stirlingshire was the first Liverpool captain to lift the First Division trophy in 1901, when they finished two points ahead of Sunderland.

The Hall of Fame also has pre-WWII places for full-back ***Donald McKinlay*** (434 appearances, 34 goals) and half-back ***Jimmy McDougall*** (356 games, 12 goals).

Then there were two centre-halves who dominated their own eras, Shankly favourite ***Ron Yeats*** signed from Dundee United and the classy ***Alan Hansen,*** who came from Partick Thistle.

Other big players for the club from north of the border were 60s stopper ***Tommy Lawrence***, FA Cup winner ***Ian St. John*** and 'Mr Consistent' ***Steve Nicol.***

As for Liverpool's greatest Scot, it's a three-way tie between the legendary ***Billy Liddell,*** the greatest player-manager ***Kenny Dalglish*** and the one and only ***Bill Shankly***.

ALAN HANSEN
STEVE NICOL
Carlsberg
adidas
NY DALGLISH
L.F.C.
BILL SHANKLY
IAN ST. JOHN

IAN CALLAGHAN MBE

'Cally', the model professional and medal collector

TOXTETH-BORN IAN CALLAGHAN MADE HIS DEBUT FOR LIVERPOOL IN 1960 AND WENT ON TO MAKE 857 APPEARANCES, STILL THE MOST EVER FOR THE CLUB.

His 18 years at Anfield saw him collect a huge haul of medals. 'Cally' was the only player to survive the journey from the Second Division to success in Europe.

"Callaghan was a key part of Bill Shankly's successful side of the 1960s."

He made his debut at Anfield in 1960 against Bristol Rovers. He was only 17 and was handed the daunting prospect of replacing the great Billy Liddell. He was applauded off the park after displaying all the elements that would mark his play in the years to come: speed, stamina and accurate crossing.

Callaghan was a key part of Bill Shankly's successful side of the 1960s, supplying the ammunition for the likes of Roger Hunt and Ian St. John.

By the 1970s he had been transformed into an energetic and classy central midfielder. In the 1973-74 season he scored his first hat-trick, surpassed Billy Liddell's appearance record and became the first Red ever to win the Football Writers' Player of the Year award. He was also given an MBE in the same year.

Although part of England's World Cup-winning squad in 1966, he only won four caps. The last of those was a surprise recall at the age of 35 in 1977.

Callaghan was the epitome of the 'model professional' who only received one yellow card in those 861 games for club and country. He left Anfield for Swansea in 1978.

LIVERPOOL FANCY DRESS PARTY -1 AUGUST 1977 - LIVERPOOL'S KEVIN KEEGAN AND JOHN TOSHACK DRESSED AS ROBIN AND BATMAN.

THE 1970s

EUROPEAN CUP - FINAL - LIVERPOOL V BORUSSIA MONCHENGLADBACH - OLYMPIC STADIUM , ROME - 25 MAY 1977.
RAY KENNEDY, JIMMY CASE AND TEAM-MATES CELEBRATE WITH THE EUROPEAN CUP TROPHY.

AT THE START OF THE 1970S LIVERPOOL DID NOT LOOK LIKE A TEAM THAT WOULD GO ON TO WIN MULTIPLE TROPHIES ACROSS SEVEN SEASONS OF THE DECADE.

They finished the 1969-70 season in fifth, 15 points adrift of Everton and were knocked out of the FA Cup by Second Division Watford.

It proved to manager Bill Shankly that he had to rebuild his squad and he quickly began the process. After a few years on the sidelines, Emlyn Hughes became a regular and goalkeeper Ray Clemence took over from Tommy Lawrence.

In 1970-71 Liverpool again finished fifth. Arsenal won the double after beating The Reds 1-2 in the FA Cup final.

Never one to miss a chance to praise the travelling Kop, Shankly announced to the fans afterwards: "Yesterday at Wembley we may have lost the cup, but you people have won everything...you won over the policemen in London. You won over the London public, and it's questionable if chairman Mao of China could have arranged such a show of strength."

In the 1971-72 season new signing Kevin Keegan shone as Liverpool lost the title by a point to Derby County after a heart-wrenching 0-0 draw with Arsenal on the last day.

SEASON	DIVISION	P	W	D	L	F	A	D	POS
1970-71	Division 1	42	17	17	8	42	24	51	5th
1971-72	Division 1	42	24	9	9	64	30	57	3rd
1972-73	Division 1	42	25	10	7	72	42	60	1st
1973-74	Division 1	42	22	13	7	52	31	57	2nd
1974-75	Division 1	42	20	11	11	60	39	51	2nd

By the next season, however, Liverpool were back to their best as they won the 1973 First Division and beat Borussia Monchengladbach 3-2 over two legs to win their first European trophy, the UEFA Cup.

In 1974 Shankly repeated his trick of following a League Championship title with an FA Cup final win. Liverpool won the cup for the second time by overpowering Newcastle 3-0.

It was a huge shock when soon afterwards Bill Shankly, clearly at the height of his powers, announced his retirement and handed the reins to his assistant, Bob Paisley.

Paisley was to become Liverpool's most successful manger and in 1976 repeated Shankly's feat of winning the League title and the UEFA Cup in the same season.

Then, in 1977, it got even better as Liverpool won the title and, on a famous night in Rome, their first ever European Cup. They then became the *first British team to retain the trophy by beating Brugge at Wembley in 1978.*

Paisley won his sixth major trophy in four years as Liverpool finished top in 1978-79, eight points clear of Nottingham Forest, ending the 1970s as the team of the decade.

SEASON	DIVISION	P	W	D	L	F	A	D	POS
1975-76	Division 1	42	23	14	5	66	31	60	1st
1976-77	Division 1	42	23	11	8	62	33	57	1st
1977-78	Division 1	42	24	9	9	65	34	57	2nd
1978-79	Division 1	42	30	8	4	85	16	68	1st
1979-80	Division 1	42	25	10	7	81	30	60	1st

THE KOP

Liverpool's 12th man and their world-famous anthem

LIVERPOOL'S SUPPORTERS ARE KNOWN THROUGHOUT THE WORLD. The Kop in full flow, belting out You'll Never Walk Alone with thousands of scarves and banners held aloft, is one of the genuinely iconic sights in football.

Many football and rugby league grounds used the term 'Spion Kop' for their popular terraces in the early 20th century, a name taken from a battle in the Boer War. But it was only at Liverpool where it was mythologised and adopted by the fans themselves, who still refer to themselves as 'Koppites'.

Those Koppites are the heartbeat of the club, Bill Shankly saying: "Anfield isn't a football ground, it's more of a shrine. These people are not simply fans, they're more like members of one large extended family".

Their famous anthem is a song from the Rodgers and Hammerstein musical Carousel, first sung at Anfield in the heady days of the early 60s. Local band Gerry and The Pacemakers having made their version of the song popular in Liverpool and across the UK.

The rise of The Kop saw this and other popular songs of the time sung on the terraces for the first time. Clubs had their own traditional song or chant, but it was at Anfield that fans started singing a range of popular songs and later changed the lyrics to celebrate their team.

You'll Never Walk Alone has become so important to the club that its title even adorns the club crest and the Shankly Gates, the memorial built to honour the club's greatest manager.

> "The rise of The Kop saw this and other popular songs of the time sung on the terraces for the first time."

28 APRIL 1973 - LIVERPOOL'S PETER CORMACK CELEBRATES WINNING THE LEAGUE CHAMPIONSHIP.

LIVERPOOL WIN THEIR EIGHTH TITLE

Shankly's new boys rise to the challenge

28 APRIL 1973 - LIVERPOOL PLAYERS TOMMY SMITH AND EMLYN HUGHES PARADE THE LEAGUE CHAMPIONSHIP TROPHY AFTER THEY SECURED THE TITLE.

LIVERPOOL ENDED A SEVEN-YEAR TROPHY DROUGHT IN 1973 BY WINNING THEIR EIGHTH FIRST DIVISION TITLE.

This was a team in transition, with many of Shankly's original superstars like *Ron Yeats* and *Ian St. John* having moved on and the likes of *Emlyn Hughes* and *Kevin Keegan* now taking up the challenge.

A fantastic start to the season, when The Reds beat both Manchester clubs 2-0 and Chelsea away, was tempered by unexpected defeats at Derby and Leicester. However, back-to-back wins of 5-1 over Carlisle and 5-0 over Sheffield United in September put The Reds back on track before Christmas.

With Keegan and *John Toshack* forming a deadly partnership and scoring 13 goals each, Liverpool finally took control of a three-way battle with Arsenal and Leeds. Hughes and fellow midfielder *Phil Boersma*, also chipped in with 7 goals each.

Leeds had done well against Liverpool in recent seasons, but a first win against *Don Revie's* men in six years effectively won the title. Peter Cormack scored just after half-time and Keegan snapped up a loose ball five minutes before the end to make it 2-0.

Liverpool were left needing just a point from their last game against Leicester, which turned out to be a dull 0-0 draw.

But winning the league again was an amazing feat in a season when The Reds also won their first European trophy, playing 66 games while using just 16 players.

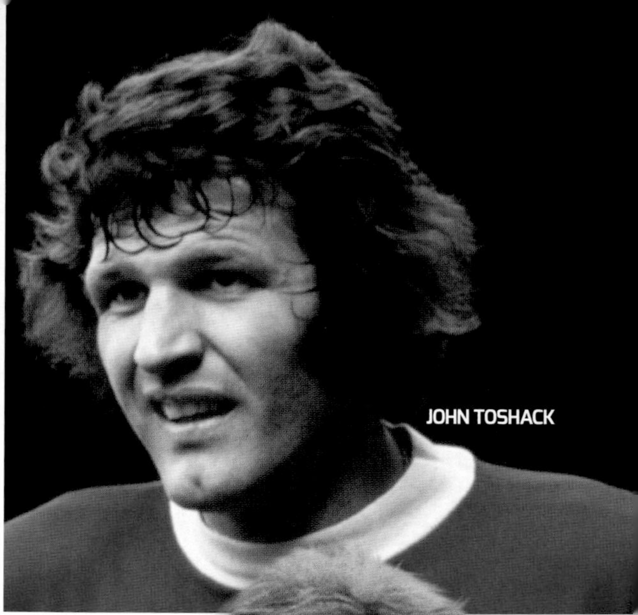

JOHN TOSHACK

KEVIN KEEGAN

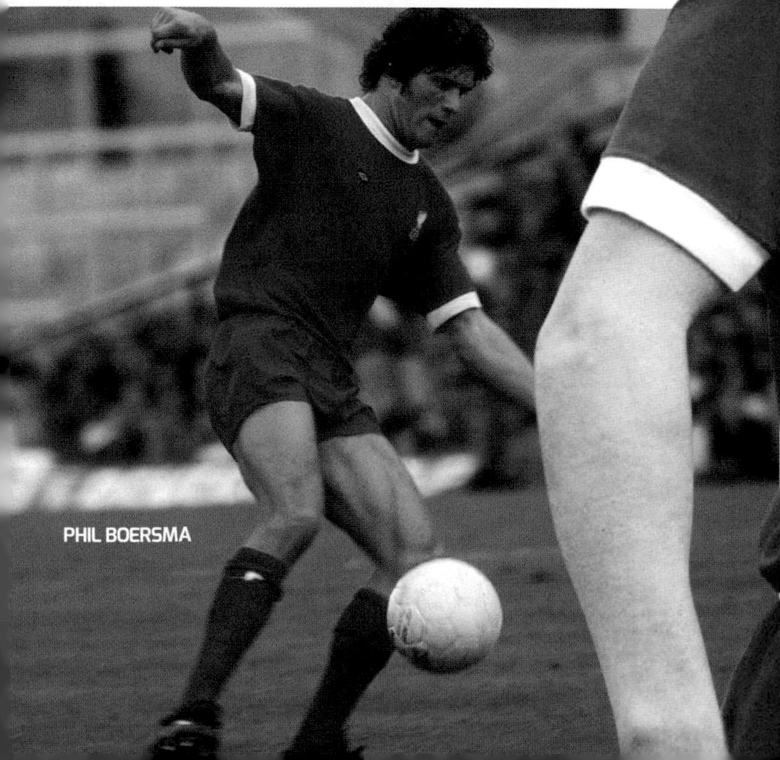

PHIL BOERSMA

LIVERPOOL WIN THE UEFA CUP IN 1973

Toshack and Keegan lead the way to The Reds' first-ever European trophy

AFTER COMING VERY CLOSE TWICE IN THE 60s, LIVERPOOL WON THEIR FIRST EUROPEAN TROPHY WHEN THEY LIFTED THE UEFA CUP IN 1973.

On the way they had to visit Germany three times, seeing off Eintracht Frankfurt 2-0, Dynamo Berlin 3-1 and Dynamo Dresden 3-0.

The semi-final was an all-English affair with Liverpool welcoming Tottenham to Anfield in the first leg. Full-back *Alec Lindsay* scored the only goal of the game to give The Reds a slim advantage to take to White Hart Lane. *Martin Peters,* 1966 World Cup hero, scored twice for Spurs, but *Steve Heighway's* away goal was enough to put Shankly's men through.

The Reds had already won the league title when they welcomed yet another German team, Borussia Monchengladbach, to Anfield for the first leg of the final. However, torrential rain meant the referee abandoned the match after 25 minutes.

With 24 hours to consider his options, Shankly played a masterstroke. Having noted during the deluge that the Germans weren't comfortable under the high ball, he brought in the towering John Toshack to replace Brian Hall. The Welshman's power in the air put two goals on a plate for Kevin Keegan. *Larry Lloyd* made it three to give The Reds a 3-0 aggregate lead.

In the second leg, Jupp Heynckes did a 'Keegan', scoring twice for Borussia, but Liverpool held on and the club had the first of many European honours.

“With 24 hours to consider his options, Shankly played a masterstroke.”

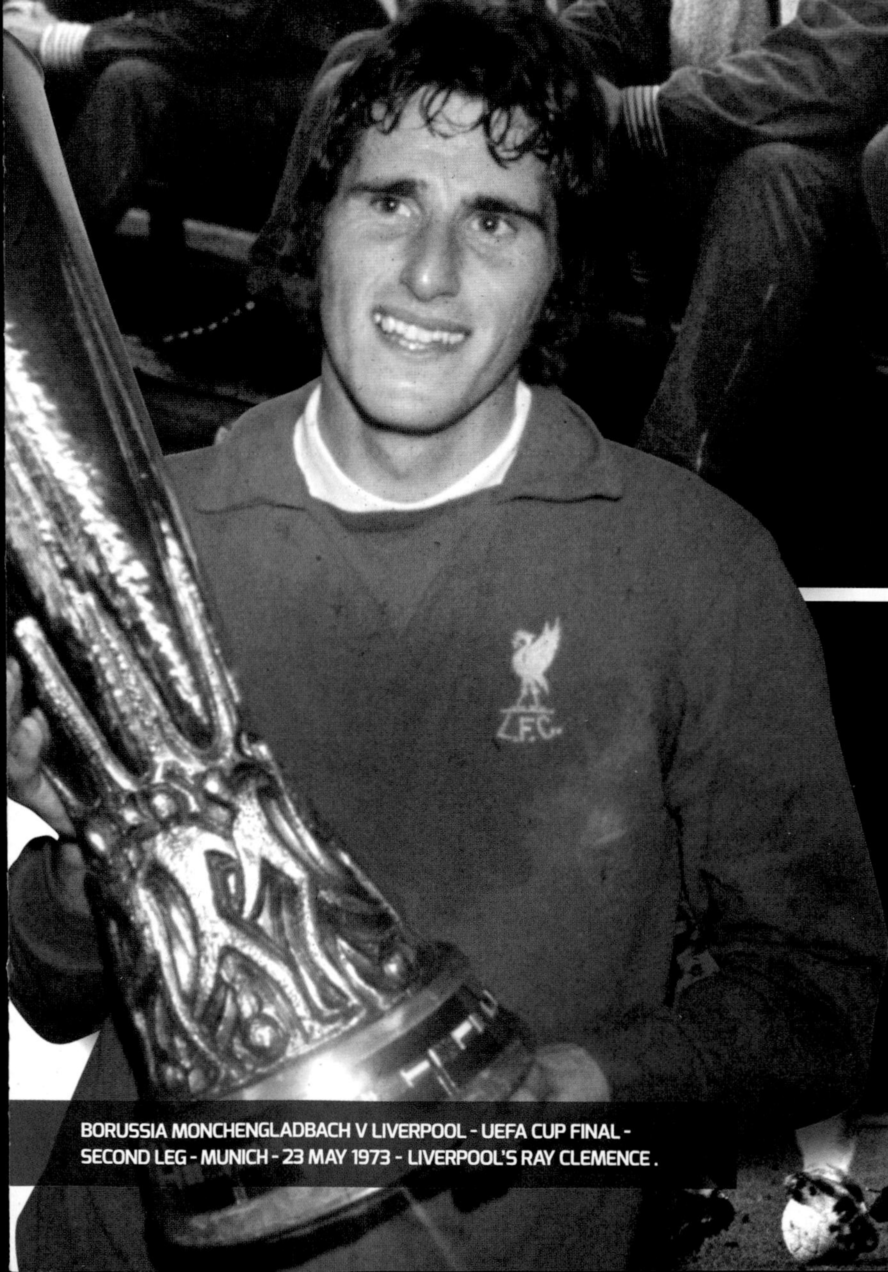

1973 UEFA CUP FINAL - FIRST LEG - LIVERPOOL V BORUSSIA MONCHENGLADBACH - ANFIELD - 10 MAY 1973 - LIVERPOOL'S STEVE HEIGHWAY.

BORUSSIA MONCHENGLADBACH V LIVERPOOL - UEFA CUP FINAL - SECOND LEG - MUNICH - 23 MAY 1973 - LIVERPOOL'S RAY CLEMENCE .

KEVIN KEEGAN

The first superstar footballer

FEW LIVERPOOL SIGNINGS HAVE EVER ATTRACTED MORE ATTENTION THAN KEVIN KEEGAN. *The pocket-rocket Yorkshireman had trials for his local club Doncaster Rovers and Jimmy Hill's Coventry City but he was unable to make the grade.*

HE EVENTUALLY SIGNED FOR SCUNTHORPE UNITED, WHERE HE WAS SPOTTED BY LEGENDARY LIVERPOOL SCOUT GEOFF TWENTYMAN.

Keegan signed for Liverpool with much fanfare in 1971, for £35,000, when he was still just 20. *Endlessly energetic and deadly in front of goal,* he soon justified the hype and made the No.7 shirt his own and turned it into an icon of the club.

He scored on his debut against Nottingham Forest after just 12 minutes and went on to net exactly 100 goals for the club in 323 games, an incredible record for a player originally marked out as a winger to replace Ian Callaghan.

Keegan scored two decisive goals in the UEFA Cup final in 1973 and two more in the FA Cup final win in 1974. *He was named Footballer of the Year and England captain in 1976.* He won 63 caps in all and scored 21 international goals.

In 1977, on the eve of a move to Hamburg and in his last game for the club, he famously ran German skipper Bertie Vogts ragged to help The Reds win their first European Cup. Upon returning from Germany, he played for both Southampton and Newcastle and scored 85 more league goals.

After hanging up his boots he managed Newcastle twice, Fulham, Manchester City and England.

LIVERPOOL WIN THE FA CUP IN 1974

Shankly bows out with Liverpool's second FA Cup

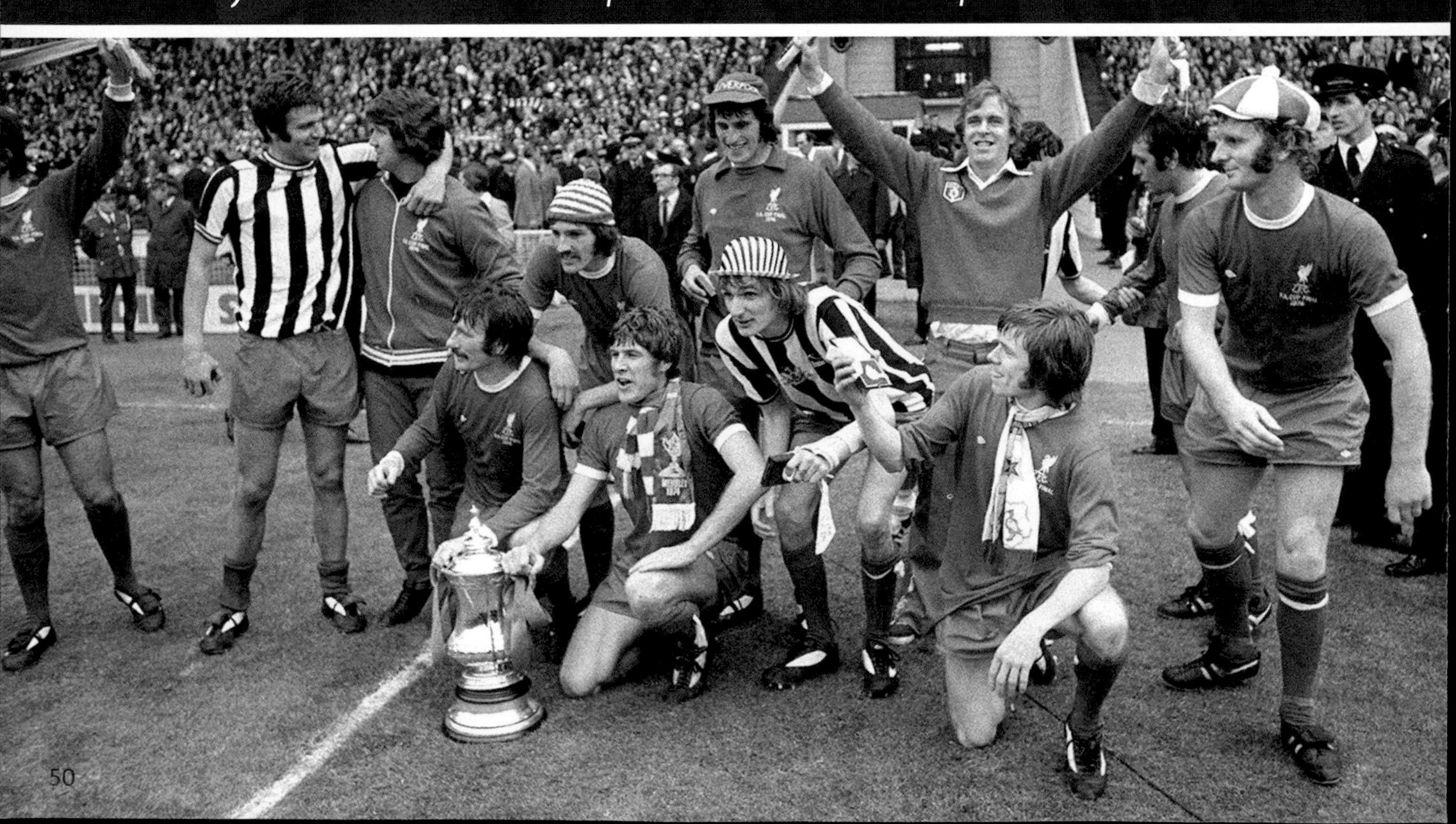

AFTER WAITING 73 YEARS TO WIN THEIR FIRST FA CUP, LIVERPOOL NEEDED ANOTHER NINE TO COLLECT THEIR NEXT.

Little did anyone know, as The Reds destroyed Newcastle United 3-0, that it would also be Bill Shankly's swansong.

Liverpool didn't start their 1973-74 FA Cup campaign looking like potential winners. Held 2-2 at Anfield by Doncaster Rovers and then by Carlisle United 0-0 in the next round, they needed successive wins in away replays to progress.

After beating Ipswich and Bristol City in the fifth and sixth rounds, Shankly's men needed another replay against Leicester City in the semi-final. Second half goals from *Brian Hall*, *Kevin Keegan* and *John Toshack* at Villa Park gave Liverpool a 3-1 win.

Newcastle United had gone into the final with their superstar striker Malcolm 'Supermac' Macdonald proclaiming that Wembley was 'his stage' and that the Geordies were the favourites.

He had scored a hat-trick against Liverpool in his first game, so he had the talent. However, his bragging was Liverpool's main motivation on the day and they made full use of it.

A tame and scoreless first half was soon eclipsed as Liverpool found top gear early in the second. Keegan scored the first off The Magpies' keeper Iam McFaul's fingertips on 58 minutes, while Toshack flicked on for *Steve Heighway* to score the second.

Liverpool then finished off the Magpies with an 11-man move as good as Wembley has seen, with Man of the match Keegan grabbing his second.

EMLYN HUGHES

Crazy horse

“The Kop nicknamed him ‘Crazy Horse’ because of his long legs, endless energy and willingness to run through a brick wall for the club.”

THE SON OF A GREAT BRITAIN RUGBY LEAGUE PLAYER, EMLYN HUGHES WAS A CUMBRIAN WITH A WELSH NAME WHO BECAME CAPTAIN OF BOTH LIVERPOOL AND ENGLAND.

He was originally bought by Bill Shankly from Blackpool as a defender but was also very versatile. Hughes' supreme fitness and never-say-die spirit saw him more usually used as a box-to-box midfielder.

He signed for Liverpool in February 1967 and went on to play 665 games for the club, winning 62 England caps. Although only 22 at the time, he was the only Liverpool man (and youngest player) in Sir Alf Ramsey's 1970 World Cup squad.

The Kop nicknamed him 'Crazy Horse' because of his long legs, endless energy and willingness to run through a brick wall for the club.

That energy was never more essential than in the double trophy-winning season of 1972-73, when he chalked up an amazing 65 games. He lifted the first of Liverpool's European Cups in 1977, the year he was also named Player of the Year by the football writers.

In all, he won eight major medals with The Reds, and then won the League Cup with Wolves after moving to Molineux in 1979. He later spent two seasons as player-manager for Rotherham United and his career ended with brief spells at Hull, Mansfield and Swansea.

Hughes still had one trick left up his sleeve, however, becoming a mainstay of the popular BBC TV series A Question of Sport.

SPOTLIGHT ON: THE DERBY

The longest-running top level derby in English football

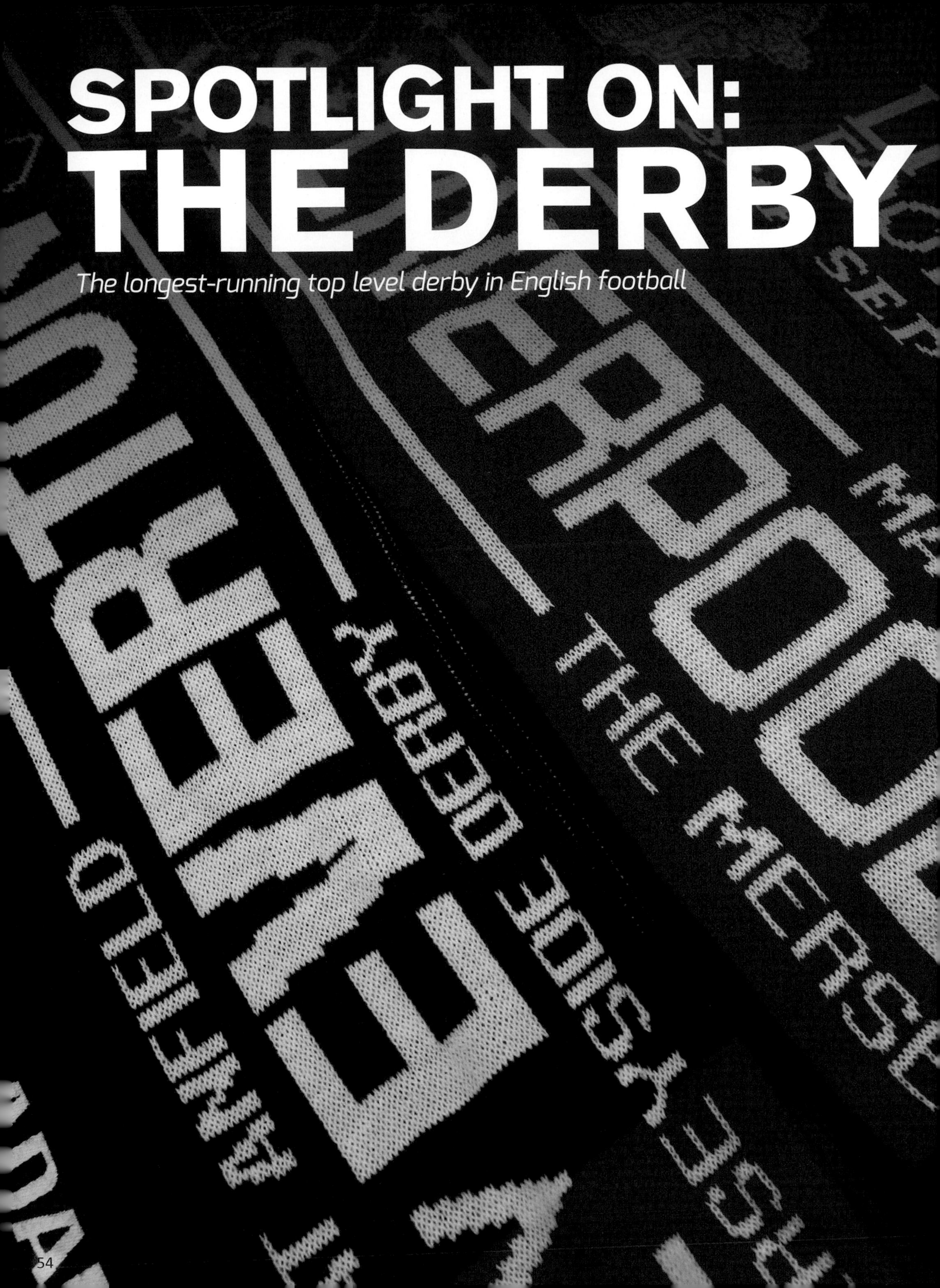

LIVERPOOL HAVE HAD MANY FIERCE AND COMPETITIVE RIVALRIES WITH OTHER CLUBS OVER THE YEARS. *A long-running feud with Manchester United is probably the best known, though in the 60s and 70s Leeds United were the team to beat, with Nottingham Forest popping up in the 80s.*

There is no rivalry like a local rivalry, however, and the fact Liverpool Football Club was formed as an off-shoot of their biggest foes Everton always gives the longest-running top flight derby in England added spice.

At the time of writing Liverpool have the whip hand, currently dominating with 88 wins to Everton's 66. There have also been 70 draws, showing how closely contested the games always are.

There has never been a season without either Liverpool or Everton in the First Division, and the city is the most successful in England with a combined total of 27 league championship titles.

The first-ever derby was in the Liverpool Senior Cup in 1893, with The Reds winning 1-0, although Everton won the first League and professional derby in 1894-95. Liverpool's first win came in the 1897-98 season, when they won 3-1 at Anfield.

Liverpool hold most of the aces. They have the largest victory, a 6-0 win at home in 1935, and three wins out of three in major finals.

The all-time top scorer in derbies is Ian Rush with 25, while Liverpool's Ray Clemence and Everton's Neville Southall share the record of 15 clean sheets.

1984 LEAGUE CUP FINAL - LIVERPOOL V EVERTON - WEMBLEY STADIUM - 25 MARCH 1984 - EVERTON'S KEVIN RICHARDSON AND LIVERPOOL'S MARK LAWRENSON CHASE THE BALL.

LIVERPOOL V EVERTON - BARCLAYS PREMIER LEAGUE - ANFIELD - 28 JANUARY 2014 - LIVERPOOL'S DANIEL STURRIDGE CELEBRATES SCORING THEIR THIRD GOAL WITH MARTN SKRTEL (TOP), LUIS SUAREZ, JON FLANAGAN (L) AND TEAM MATES.

LIVERPOOL V EVERTON - LEAGUE DIVISION ONE - ANFIELD - 31 DECEMBER 1966 - EVERTON'S ALAN BALL (C) AGAINST LIVERPOOL'S RON YEATS (L) AND TOMMY SMITH (R).

LIVERPOOL WIN THE FIRST DIVISION AND UEFA CUP IN 1976

Paisley comes up trumps in his second season

UEFA CUP FINAL SECOND LEG - MAY 1976 - CLUB BRUGGE 1 LIVERPOOL 1 (LIVERPOOL WIN 4-3 ON AGGREGATE) - KEVIN KEEGAN AND JOHN TOSHACK OF LIVERPOOL CELEBRATE THEIR WIN IN THE FINAL .

BOB PAISLEY'S FIRST SEASON IN CHARGE OF THE REDS HAD ENDED QUIETLY BY THEIR STANDARDS, WITH ONLY A FIRST DIVISION RUNNERS-UP PLACE TO SHOW FOR THEIR ENDEAVOURS.

The 1975-76 season, however, provec that Paisley had been the right choice as manager.

A 3-2 comeback win against Spurs in the third game proved the catalyst for another double trophy-winning season. After being beaten at home by Middlesbrough in March, they went on a 14-match unbeaten run.

John Toshack's 23 goals enabled Paisley's team to build the momentum which saw them win eight of their last nine matches.

An intense period of games saw The Reds end the league season at Molineux sandwiched between the two legs of the UEFA Cup final. ***A famous 3-1 win relegated Wolves and broke Queens Park Rangers' hearts as The Reds beat them to the title by just one point.***

In the UEFA Cup, John Toshack had scored the only goal of a famous semi-final win in the Nou Camp against Barcelona, meaning a 1-1 draw at Anfield was enough to see them through to the final against FC Brugge.

Liverpool were 2-0 down at half-time at home in the first leg, but came back to win 3-2 with goals from ***Ray Kennedy***, ***Jimmy Case*** and ***Kevin Keegan***. A 1-1 draw in Belgium, thanks to another crucial Keegan goal, secured the UEFA Cup for a second time.

WOLVERHAMPTON WANDERERS V LIVERPOOL - MOLINEUX - 4 MAY 1976 - LIVERPOOL'S RAY CLEMENCE AND DAVID FAIRCLOUGH CELEBRATE AFTER WINNING THE CHAMPIONSHIP .

WOLVERHAMPTON WANDERERS V LIVERPOOL - MOLINEUX - 4 MAY 1976 - LIVERPOOL'S KEVIN KEEGAN IN ACTION WITH WOLVES' MIKE BAILEY.

1976 UEFA CUP FINAL - SECOND LEG - CLUB BRUGGE V LIVERPOOL - OLYMPIC STADIUM - 19 MAY 1976 - LIVERPOOL'S RAY KENNEDY , JIMMY CASE AND PHIL NEAL CELEBRATE WITH THE TROPHY.

LIVERPOOL WIN THE EUROPEAN CUP IN 1977

The first of five caps a double-winning season

IF 1976 HAD BEEN AN AMAZING YEAR FOR THE REDS, 1977 WOULD BE OUT OF THIS WORLD AS BOB PAISLEY'S MEN CLAIMED THEIR 10TH LEAGUE TITLE AND WON THEIR FIRST EUROPEAN CUP.

The Championship was won on the back of impressive form at Anfield, with 18 wins and no defeats from their 21 home games. Three of those home wins against Arsenal, Ipswich Town and Manchester United left The Reds needing just three points from their last four matches.

1977 EUROPEAN CUP FINAL - LIVERPOOL V BORUSSIA MONCHENGLADBACH - OLYMPIC STADIUM - ROME - 25 MAY 1977 - LIVERPOOL'S JIMMY CASE , PHIL NEAL AND TOMMY SMITH CELEBRATE WITH THE TROPHY.

EUROPEAN CUP - FINAL - LIVERPOOL V BORUSSIA MONCHENGLADBACH - OLYMPIC STADIUM, ROME - 25 MAY 1977 - JIMMY CASE AND PHIL NEAL KISS THE EUROPEAN CUP TROPHY.

KEVIN CALLAGHAN AND MANAGER BOB PAISLEY CELEBRATE AFTER LIVERPOOL BEAT BORUSSIA MONCHENGLADBACH IN THE EUROPEAN CUP FINAL 1977.

A 0-0 draw with West Ham clinched the title, though it was a close-run thing again with Manchester City finishing runners-up, just one point behind The Reds.

Once again, the dynamic duo of *Kevin Keegan* and *John Toshack* had provided the most goals with 22 between them.

Liverpool then went into the European Cup final on a downer after losing the FA Cup final 2-1 to old foes Manchester United.

But it had been an amazing season in Europe with some unforgettable performances, the David Fairclough-inspired comeback against St. Etienne the pinnacle.

So confidence was high as thousands of fans travelled to Rome for what was to be Kevin Keegan's last game for the club. It was German champions Borussia Monchengladbach who stood in the way again.

That confidence proved to be well-founded as goals from *Terry McDermott*, *Tommy Smith* (in his 600th game) and a penalty from *Phil Neal* made the final score 3-1, enabling *Emlyn Hughes* to lift the trophy and light up the Olympic Stadium with his huge grin.

1977 EUROPEAN CUP FINAL - LIVERPOOL V BORUSSIA MONCHENGLADBACH - OLYMPIC STADIUM - ROME - 25 MAY 1977 - LIVERPOOL FANS ON THE TERRACES.

BOB PAISLEY

The man with the Midas touch

BOB PAISLEY WAS WITHOUT DOUBT LIVERPOOL'S MOST SUCCESSFUL MANAGER. *With the well-shaped lump of clay given him by Bill Shankly, this humble Durham miner's son moulded an almost unstoppable team which would go on to dominate English football for years.*

> **"Liverpool fans will forever be thankful for that change of heart."**

7/5/83 ENGLISH LEAGUE DIVISION ONE MATCH AT ANFIELD. LIVERPOOL 1 ASTON VILLA 1. LIVERPOOL MANAGER BOB PAISLEY HOLDS THE LEAGUE CHAMPIONSHIP TROPHY ALOFT AS THE CLUB WIN THE TITLE AT ANFIELD IN HIS LAST EVER SEASON IN CHARGE OF THE CLUB.

Paisley arrived at Anfield in 1939, beginning an association of nearly 50 years with the club. He then served in World War Two in a tank brigade, seeing fierce action at Tobruk, El-Alamein and the liberation of Rome.

He was given his debut in 1947 by manager George Kay in the same match as Billy Liddell, and played 253 times for the club. ***He retired from playing in 1954 and for most players that would have been it, but Paisley simply didn't want to leave Anfield.*** He had unfinished business.

He became a self-taught physiotherapist and coached the reserves until Bill Shankly wisely made him his assistant manager in 1959. When Shankly retired unexpectedly in 1974 the Liverpool board only had one man in mind as a replacement. Paisley, however, was initially reluctant due to his taciturn nature. But he knew he could rely on solid 'Boot Room' support from Joe Fagan and Reuben Bennett, so eventually took the job.

Liverpool fans will forever be thankful for that change of heart as Paisley racked up a staggering 20 trophies in just nine years, at a rate of more than two per season. ***He and Carlo Ancelotti are the only managers to have won three European Cups.***

NOVEMBER 1969 - INJURED LIVERPOOL PLAYER TOMMY SMITH RECEIVES TREATMENT FROM BOB PAISLEY IN THE TREATMENT ROOM.

APRIL 1968 - LIVERPOOL TRAINER BOB PAISLEY CARRIES OFF FULL-BACK EMLYN HUGHES.

1977 - BOB PAISLEY, FORMER MANAGER OF LIVERPOOL FC, WITH THE EUROPEAN CUP AND THE FOOTBALL LEAGUE CHAMPIONSHIP TROPHY DURING A VISIT TO HIS HOME TOWN OF HETTON.

LIVERPOOL WIN THE EUROPEAN CUP AGAIN IN 1978

Reds are the first British team to retain the trophy

LIVERPOOL MOVED SWIFTLY TO REPLACE THE TALISMANIC KEVIN KEEGAN IN 1977 AND IN 1978 KENNY DALGLISH, THE NEW 'KING OF THE KOP' SCORED THE GOAL WHICH MADE THEM THE FIRST BRITISH TEAM TO RETAIN THE EUROPEAN CUP.

The goal was the new No.7's 30th for the season, and the final was against old European rivals and Belgian champions FC Brugge. The venue was Wembley, where just as they had in Rome a year before, the travelling Kop dominated the ground and roared their team to victory in a surprisingly dour encounter.

The road to Wembley had seen another old foe dispatched in the semis, as once again Borussia Monchengladbach were Liverpool's victims. The Germans must have been dreading the draw every time their name went into the hat with The Reds. Dynamo Dresden and Benfica had also been beaten on the way, 6-3 and 6-2 respectively on aggregate.

The final saw Brugge's Danish keeper Birger Jensen in fine form, thwarting all Liverpool's early attempts with *Graeme Souness* and *David Fairclough* both going close. But one piece of magic in the 65th minute broke the deadlock. An incisive through ball from Graeme Souness led to a sublime *Dalglish* chip over *Jensen*.

It was a typical Dalglish goal, a match-winner conjured from almost nothing. Liverpool won 1-0 and beaming skipper *Emlyn Hughes* lifted the European Cup for the second time in a row.

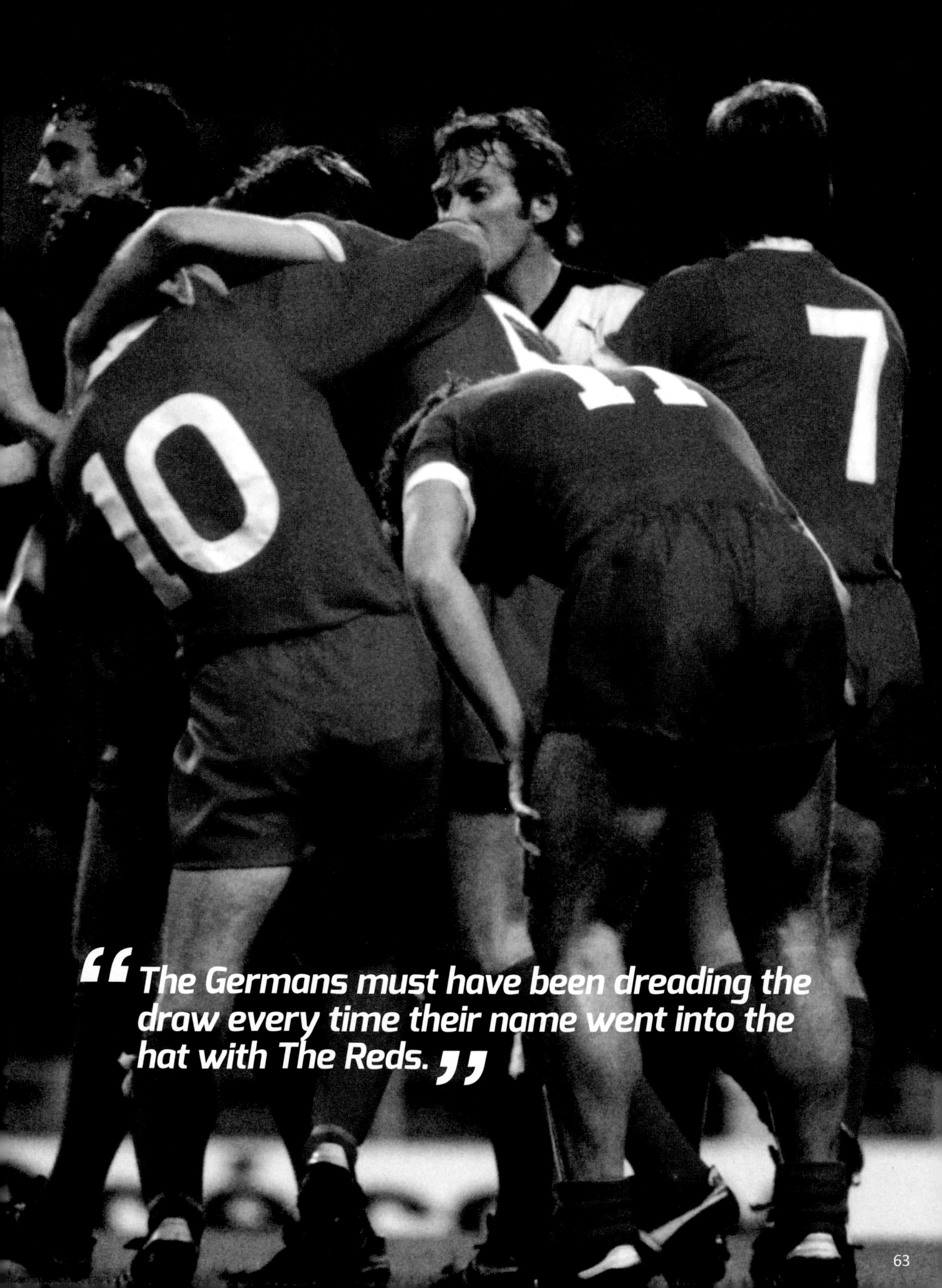

"The Germans must have been dreading the draw every time their name went into the hat with The Reds."

LIVERPOOL WIN THE FIRST DIVISION IN 1979

Title back at Anfield for the 11th time

LIVERPOOL WON THE FIRST DIVISION TITLE IN 1979 WITH 68 POINTS, A FOOTBALL LEAGUE RECORD FOR THE OLD TWO POINTS FOR A WIN SYSTEM. *They also scored 85 goals and only conceded 16 to finish with an incredible goal difference of 69. Fortress Anfield was once again the foundation for the title win as The Reds won 19 times and drew twice, losing none at home.*

" Paisley's side started the season with six straight wins, including a 7-0 demolition of Spurs. "

ALAN KENNEDY

Graeme Souness says it was the greatest team he ever played in, with the likes of Ray Kennedy and Terry McDermott at the peak of their powers. Once again Kenny Dalglish led the scoring with 21 league goals, ably assisted by David Johnson with 16.

Paisley's side started the season with six straight wins, including a 7-0 demolition of Spurs. It was as if they were only interested in the league, however, as they went out of the League Cup to Sheffield United and then just as quickly out of the European Cup.

Brian Clough had created a team in Nottingham Forest which could almost match The Reds. Forest won 2-0 on aggregate before going on to win the trophy, keeping it in England for a third consecutive year.

Liverpool lost 3-1 at Aston Villa in April, conceding three goals in game for the first time in 15 months, but it was just a blip.

Fittingly, the 11th title was wrapped up with a 3-0 home win against Villa on May 8 with *Alan Kennedy, Kenny Dalglish* and *Terry McDermott* grabbing the goals.

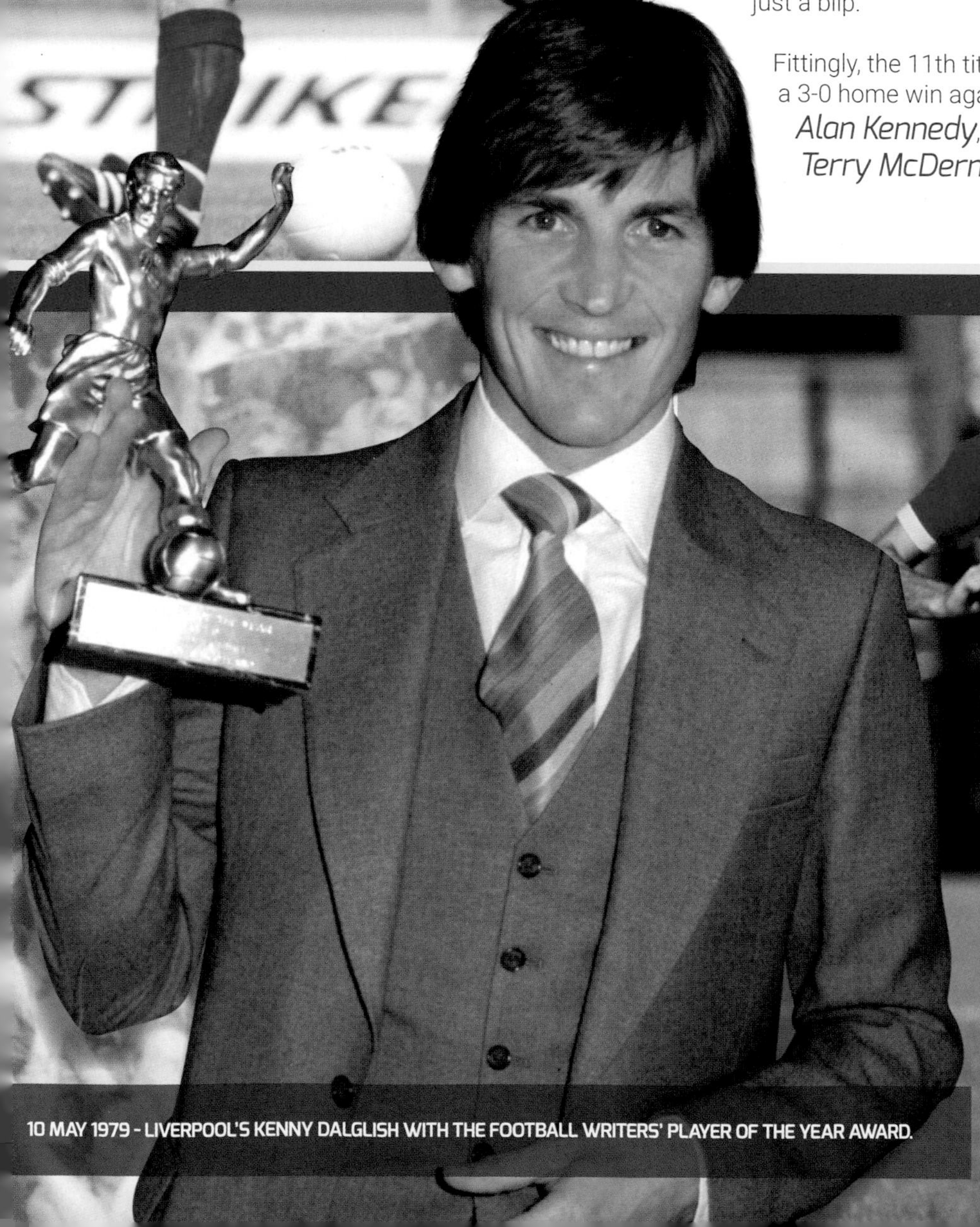

RAY KENNEDY

10 MAY 1979 - LIVERPOOL'S KENNY DALGLISH WITH THE FOOTBALL WRITERS' PLAYER OF THE YEAR AWARD.

RAY CLEMENCE

Liverpool's Mr. Reliable between the sticks

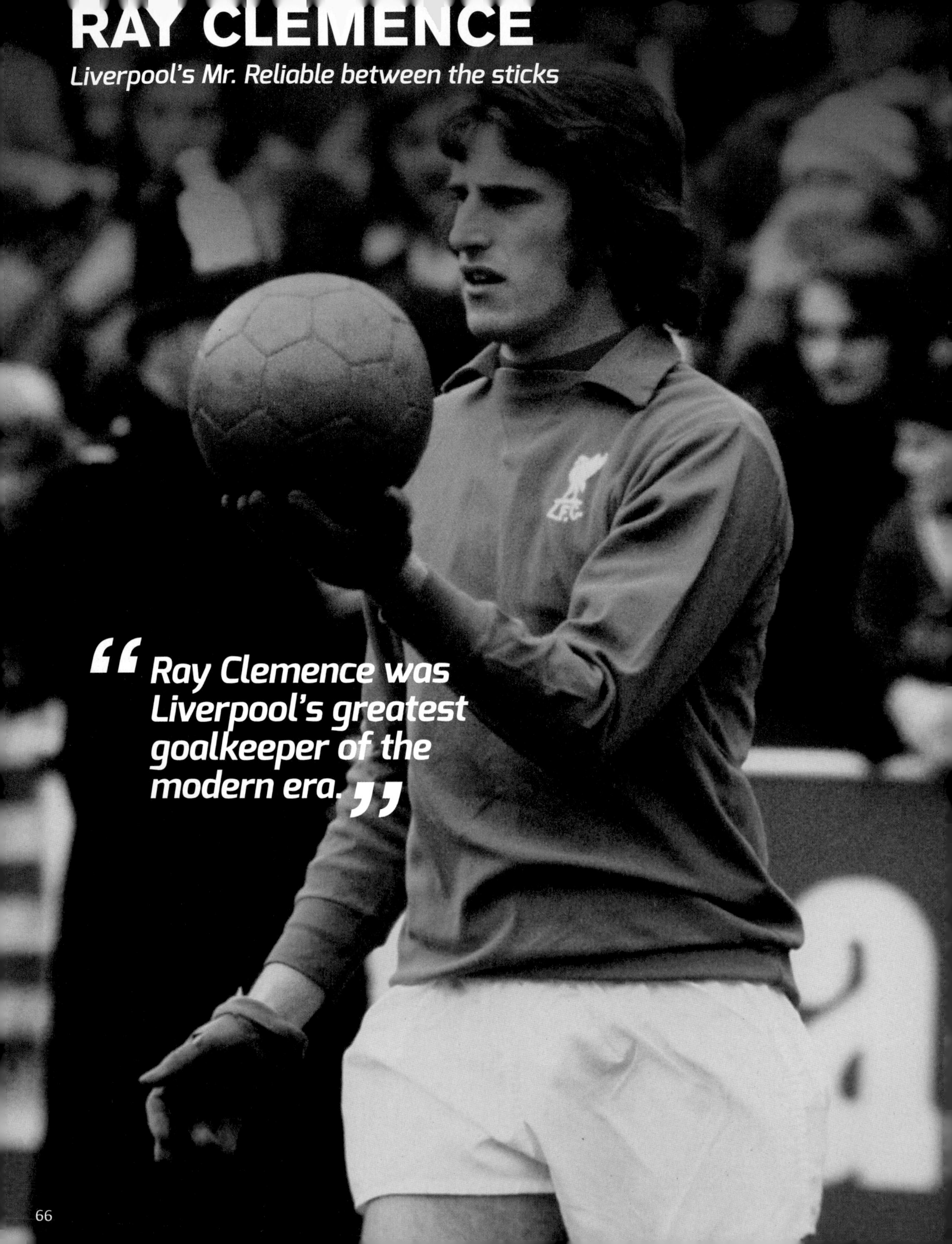

> *"Ray Clemence was Liverpool's greatest goalkeeper of the modern era."*

RAY CLEMENCE WAS LIVERPOOL'S GREATEST GOALKEEPER OF THE MODERN ERA, AND IS THIRD BEHIND IAN CALLAGHAN AND JAMIE CARRAGHER IN THE LIST OF APPEARANCES.

Born in Skegness, he played for Scunthorpe United (where Kevin Keegan had started) until he was brought to Anfield by Bill Shankly in 1967. Clemence had a frustrating two years in the reserves before finally replacing Tommy Lawrence in the 1969-70 season.

He'd made his debut in 1968 in a League Cup game against Swansea, but didn't play again until the two legs of a 14-0 aggregate win over Dundalk in the Fairs (UEFA) Cup. He missed just six league games in the next 11 seasons.

In 1970-71 he let in just 22 goals in 41 games, and then in 1978-79 smashed that record by only conceding 16 in a season when he kept 28 clean sheets in all.

He played 665 games for The Reds and won 61 England caps.

His last game came, fittingly, with both a clean sheet and a major trophy as Liverpool beat Real Madrid to win the European Cup in Paris in 1981.

At the age of 32 he moved to Tottenham, winning the FA Cup with them in his first season. He kept the No.1 jersey at Spurs for seven years, playing 240 games.

'Clem' won five Championships, an FA Cup, a League Cup, three European Cups and two UEFA Cups with The Reds. He also won another UEFA Cup with Spurs.

THE 1980s

15 MAY 1982 - LIVERPOOL MANAGER BOB PAISLEY CELEBRATES WITH A GLASS OF CHAMPAGNE IN THE DRESSING ROOM AT ANFIELD AFTER HIS TEAM HAD WON THE LEAGUE CHAMPIONSHIP FOR A RECORD 13TH TIME AFTER A 3-1 VICTORY OVER SPURS.

1983 LEAGUE CUP FINAL - LIVERPOOL V MANCHESTER UNITED - WEMBLEY STADIUM - 26 MARCH 1983 - LIVERPOOL'S ALAN HANSEN AND GRAEME SOUNESS CELEBRATE WITH THE TROPHY.

LIVERPOOL STARTED THE DECADE AS THEY MEANT TO GO ON, IN UNSTOPPABLE FORM, BY RETAINING THE FIRST DIVISION TITLE, TWO POINTS AHEAD OF MANCHESTER UNITED.

In 1981, a 1-2 defeat to Leicester was significant as it was the first time in 85 games that Liverpool had lost at home, ending a record of 69 wins and 16 draws.

It hardly mattered, however, as *Paisley's men won the European Cup again.* It was won for the third time after a 1-0 win over Real Madrid in Paris. The Reds also won the League Cup for the first time after a replay against West Ham.

That year, Bill Shankly passed away after a heart attack and the club erected The Shankly Gates as a permanent memorial to the man who made Liverpool famous across the world.

In 1982 The Reds were back in title-winning form, winning 20 of 25 league games to see off runners-up Ipswich Town. They also retained the League Cup, beating Spurs 2-1 at Wembley.

The 1980s were only three years old when Paisley celebrated his seventh major trophy of the decade, as Liverpool landed the double double of League title and League Cup again in 1983.

SEASON	DIVISION	P	W	D	L	F	A	D	POS
1980-81	Division 1	42	17	17	8	62	42	51	5th
1981-82	Division 1	42	26	9	7	80	32	87	1st
1982-83	Division 1	42	24	10	8	87	37	82	1st
1983-84	Division 1	42	22	14	6	73	32	80	1st
1984-85	Division 1	42	22	11	9	68	35	77	2nd

The League Cup win was significant in Bob Paisley's last game in charge, as the victory over Manchester United gave captain Graeme Souness the opportunity to allow Paisley the honour of climbing the Wembley steps to lift the trophy himself.

In 1983-84 Paisley's successor, 'Smokin' Joe Fagan, won a remarkable treble. First Liverpool landed their fourth successive League Cup in the first ever all-Merseyside final at Wembley.

They then won the League title again by three points from Southampton, and followed that up by beating AS Roma on penalties in their own stadium to win their fourth European Cup.

The tragedy of Heysel the next season ended Fagan's brief but marvellous reign as manager, and sadly haunted him for the rest of his life.

In 1985 Kenny Dalglish became the first player-manager in the First Division, and promptly scored the winning goal against Chelsea to win the title.

The next year Dalglish delivered the double, as his team pipped Everton to both the League and FA Cup.

In 1988 The Reds won the League again, but Wimbledon's shock FA Cup win prevented another amazing double.

Although Liverpool won the FA Cup in 1989, the decade ended with the horror of the Hillsborough disaster. The 96 fans who simply went to a football match and never came back that day will always be remembered by the club.

SEASON	DIVISION	P	W	D	L	F	A	D	POS
1985-86	Division 1	42	26	10	6	89	37	88	1st
1986-87	Division 1	42	23	8	11	72	42	77	2nd
1987-88	Division 1	42	26	12	2	87	24	90	1st
1988-89	Division 1	42	22	10	6	65	28	76	2nd
1989-90	Division 1	38	23	10	5	78	37	79	1st

RAY KENNEDY

THE player of the 1970s

> *"Kennedy was told by Port Vale manager Stanley Matthews that he was 'too slow to be a footballer'."*

DESCRIBED BY PUNDIT JIMMY GREAVES AS 'THE PLAYER OF THE 1970S', AT THE AGE OF 16, RAY KENNEDY WAS TOLD BY PORT VALE MANAGER STANLEY MATTHEWS THAT HE WAS "TOO SLOW TO BE A FOOTBALLER".

He was spotted playing amateur football by Arsenal and played 158 times for them. He won the Fairs (UEFA) Cup in 1969-70 and the double in 1970-71 (sealed with a 2-1 win over Liverpool in the FA Cup final).

Kennedy signed for The Reds on the same day as Bill Shankly announced his retirement in 1974. At Arsenal he had been a free-scoring centre forward, but Bob Paisley had other plans.

He scored on his debut in the 1974-75 season in a 3-0 win over Chelsea. Paisley made him an attacking left-sided midfielder and he was a key part of the successful Reds sides of the 70s.

He scored crucial goals in the UEFA Cup final in 1976 and against Bayern Munich in the European Cup semi-final in 1981.

Kennedy was unlucky to win just 17 caps for his country, as he played for England under Ron Greenwood, who preferred West Ham's Trevor Brooking on the left.

After 393 games he moved to Swansea in 1982, where old team-mate John Toshack was boss. At the end of his first season, Toshack accused Kennedy of not trying and he left The Swans.

What nobody knew until later was that Kennedy was suffering from Parkinson's disease which he continues to fight at the time of writing.

LIVERPOOL RETAIN THE LEAGUE AGAIN

Paisley delivers the 12th Championship

LIVERPOOL RETAINED THE FIRST DIVISION TITLE IN 1980, WINNING IT FOR A RECORD 12TH TIME. *The Reds had got off to a slow start, winning just two of their opening seven games in a run which included defeats at Southampton and Nottingham Forest.*

3 MAY 1980 - PHIL THOMPSON OF LIVERPOOL WITH LEAGUE TROPHY AFTER BEATING ASTON VILLA .

ARSENAL V LIVERPOOL - DIVISION ONE - HIGHBURY - 12 APRIL 1980 - ARSENAL'S WILLIE YOUNG IN ACTION AGAINST LIVERPOOL'S DAVID JOHNSON.

JIMMY CASE

However, a 4-0 home win over Manchester City in October turned the tide and got the engine purring. A 2-0 win over Manchester United on Boxing Day was part of a run of ten wins from 11 games which put Paisley's team in the driving seat once more.

January and February saw Liverpool take on Nottingham Forest four times in seven games in the league, League Cup and FA Cup. In all competitions against Brian Clough's side that season their record was played five, won two, lost two and drawn one.

The Reds then had to face Arsenal five times in a month as two FA Cup semi-final replays failed to produce a winner. The Gunners finally won the third reply 1-0, while the league match was a 1-1 draw.

As for Manchester United, they were not to be shaken off easily and, just as they had 12 months previously, Liverpool needed to beat Aston Villa at home to win the title.

An eventful game saw *David Johnson* open the scoring before *Avi Cohen* levelled with an own goal. The Israeli defender then turned from villain to hero by firing The Reds in front. Johnson grabbed a second and a Villa own goal made the final score 4-1 and put the trophy back in Liverpool's hands.

"A 2-0 win over Manchester United on Boxing Day was part of a run of ten wins from 11 games which put Paisley's team in the driving seat once more."

LIVERPOOL WIN LEAGUE CUP AND EUROPEAN CUP IN 1981

Paisley keeps up his incredible trophy-winning run

ALTHOUGH LIVERPOOL DIDN'T WIN THE LEAGUE IN 1981, IT WAS STILL ANOTHER SPECTACULARLY SUCCESSFUL SEASON WITH TWO MORE TROPHIES FOR BOB PAISLEY AND HIS TEAM. *In April came their first ever League Cup win, a trophy they would go on to almost own over the next few years. Then there was the small matter of their third European Cup triumph.*

1981 EUROPEAN CUP FINAL - LIVERPOOL V REAL MADRID - PARC DE PRINCES - PARIS - 27 MAY 1981 - LIVERPOOL'S PHIL NEAL AND GOALSCORER ALAN KENNEDY CELEBRATE WITH THE TROPHY.

Despite beginning their League Cup campaign with a 1-0 defeat to lowly Bradford City at Valley Parade, Liverpool seemed determined to win the one trophy that still eluded them. They dispatched Bradford 4-0 in the home leg before beating Swindon, Portsmouth, Birmingham and Manchester City in the semi-final.

In the final, West Ham United took Liverpool all the way. A 1-1 draw at Wembley meant a replay at Villa Park, where the unlikely figure of *Alan Hansen* grabbed the winner with a close-range finish in a 2-1 win.

In Europe, Liverpool had handed Oulun Palloseura of Finland a 10-1 drubbing at Anfield at the start of the campaign and seen off Bayern Munich in the semis.

The mighty Real Madrid faced The Reds in the European Cup final in Paris, but another tense game saw Liverpool emerge victorious. Popular left-back *Alan Kennedy*, aka 'Barney Rubble', was another unlikely hero as the game's only goalscorer.

Skipper and proud Scouser *Phil Thompson* lifted the trophy, just as he had that first League Cup in April.

29 MAY 1981 - THE LIVERPOOL FC TOUR BUS PASSES THROUGH LIVERPOOL CITY CENTRE AS THE PLAYERS ENJOY A PARADE IN THEIR HONOUR AFTER WINNING THE 1981 EUROPEAN CUP FINAL AGAINST REAL MADRID (1-0).

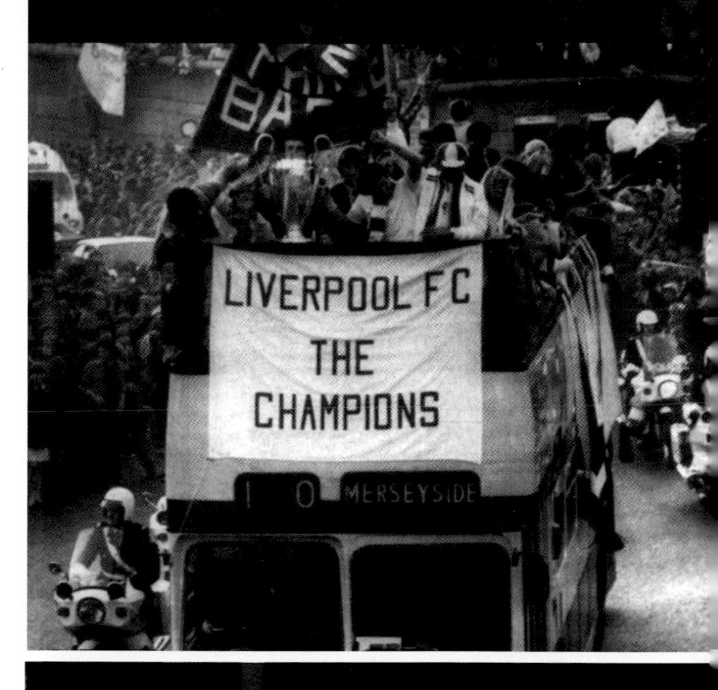

1981 LEAGUE CUP FINAL - REPLAY - LIVERPOOL V WEST HAM UNITED - VILLA PARK - 6 APRIL 1981 - LIVERPOOL'S ALAN HANSEN (OUT OF FRAME) SCORES THE SECOND GOAL AS KENNY DALGLISH LOOKS ON.

LIVERPOOL V REAL MADRID - EUROPEAN CUP FINAL - PARIS - 28 MAY 1981 - LIVERPOOL PLAYERS PHIL THOMPSON AND ALAN KENNEDY CELEBRATE WITH THE EUROPEAN CUP AFTER THEIR VICTORY OVER REAL MADRID IN PARIS.

1981 LEAGUE CUP FINAL - REPLAY - LIVERPOOL V WEST HAM UNITED - VILLA PARK - 6 APRIL 1981 - LIVERPOOL'S PHIL THOMPSON LIFTS THE TROPHY.

THE DOUBLE-DOUBLE YEARS

1981 - 1983

Liverpool win League and League Cup together two seasons in a row

LIVERPOOL CLAIMED A UNIQUE DOUBLE-DOUBLE IN THE 1981-82 AND 1982-83 SEASONS AS THEY RETAINED BOTH THE FIRST DIVISION TITLE AND THE LEAGUE CUP BOTH TIMES.

They booked their passage to the 1982 League Cup final in its first season as The Milk Cup after beating Arsenal in the semis. They beat Tottenham in the final 3-1 in extra-time, with new boy Ronnie Whelan grabbing a brace.

1983 LEAGUE CUP FINAL - LIVERPOOL V MANCHESTER UNITED - WEMBLEY STADIUM - 26 MARCH 1983 - LIVERPOOL'S ALAN HANSEN AND GRAEME SOUNESS LEAD THE PARADE.

The Reds' 13th league title came in Ian Rush's second season, who, after a slow start to his Anfield career, netted 30 times. Liverpool's 4-0 win over runners-up Ipswich Town was the pick of Liverpool's fine season.

In 1983 Liverpool suffered a miserable February, losing to Burnley 0-1 in the League Cup semi-final first leg then 1-2 to Brighton at home in the FA Cup. This was soon followed by a 0-2 defeat at Widzew Lodz in the European Cup. Fortunately, they'd won the League Cup semi-final first leg against Burnley 3-0.

A 2-1 win over Manchester United at Wembley saw Liverpool retain The Milk Cup with *Alan Kennedy* and *Ronnie 'The Milk Cup kid' Whelan* scoring the goals.

The 1983 League Championship win was significant as it was Bob Paisley's last. Liverpool strolled to the title, finishing 11 points clear of unlikely but deserved runners-up Watford.

Ian Rush made another remarkable contribution, his own high point coming in the derby at Goodison Park where he scored four goals in an historic 5-0 win over The Toffees.

1983 LEAGUE CUP FINAL - LIVERPOOL V MANCHESTER UNITED - WEMBLEY STADIUM - 26 MARCH 1983 - LIVERPOOL'S IAN RUSH GETS BETWEEN RAY WILKINS AND KEVIN MORAN.

1982 LEAGUE CUP FINAL - LIVERPOOL V TOTTENHAM HOTSPUR - WEMBLEY STADIUM - 13 MARCH 1982 - LIVERPOOL'S MARK LAWRENSON , RONNIE WHELAN AND BRUCE GROBBELAAR CELEBRATE WITH THE TROPHY.

JOE FAGAN

Genial Joe's short but sweet reign as manager

JUST AS BOB PAISLEY HAD BEEN UNDER BILL SHANKLY, JOE FAGAN WAS A QUIETLY EFFICIENT PRESENCE AT MANAGER BOB PAISLEY'S SIDE, *so it came as no surprise when Paisley's successor was another 'Boot Room' graduate.*

A SCOUSER WHO HAD PLAYED 158 GAMES FOR MANCHESTER CITY AND THEN NON-LEAGUE FOOTBALL FOR NELSON, BRADFORD PARK AVENUE AND ALTRINCHAM, HE JOINED THE COACHING STAFF AT LIVERPOOL IN 1958.

Before joining City, he had fought in World War Two just like Paisley. Fagan volunteered for the Navy and was a telegraphist in a minesweeping flotilla stationed in Egypt.

As coach of the reserve team, Fagan was responsible for the development of key players like Roger Hunt, Ian Callaghan and Tommy Smith, so when he had to start rebuilding the squad in 1983, the Liverpool board had full confidence in him.

In his first season in charge, in 1983-84, Fagan took Liverpool back to the Stadio Olimpico in Rome - this time to face AS Roma on their home ground. He had taken the team to the verge of an unprecedented European Cup, League and League Cup treble. His team won on penalties and Joe had emulated his great friend Bob Paisley in his first season.

The next season ended in disaster for both genial Joe, Liverpool Football Club and especially Juventus Football Club at the Heysel Stadium in Brussels. Fagan had already announced his retirement, but witnessing that terrible tragedy at his last match as manager left him a haunted man, barely able to talk about his wonderful triumphs.

SPOTLIGHT ON:

Liverpool's control centre and breeding ground for success

FROM THE 1960S TO THE 1990S, LIVERPOOL'S NERVE CENTRE AND TACTICAL HUB WAS A HUMBLE STOREROOM AT THEIR MELWOOD TRAINING GROUND.

The tiny room, which was used to store the players' boots, became a common room for the coaching staff to relax and discuss tactics, players and other issues.

There is some debate as to whether the Boot Room was presided over by Bill Shankly, but certainly his trusted lieutenants made it theirs.

Future managers *Joe Fagan, Bob Paisley, Ronnie Moran* and *Roy Evans* were joined by club stalwarts *Reuben Bennett* and *Tom Saunders* to relax, chat and drink whisky or bottles of stout.

Joe Fagan's hand-written diaries discovered in a loft in 2011 reveal that he was inadvertently responsible for the Boot Room's creation. *He coached a nearby*

THE BOOT ROOM

Guinness brewery team part-time and they sent him a few crates of the black stuff.

The Boot Room was the only place to store the crates, and so the coaches would gather there to relax, drink and swap ideas.

Fagan's diaries reveal that it hardly developed into a salubrious office, but Shankly's cohorts liked it that way.

"In time it would become furnished with luxuries like a rickety old table and a couple of plastic chairs, a tatty piece of carpet on the floor and a calendar on a wall... there was little evidence to suggest this room was even part of a football club."

The Boot Room was so crucial to the club's success that it has its own place in Liverpool folklore.

LIVERPOOL MANAGER BILL SHANKLY (LEFT) AND HIS NEW TEAM OF BACKROOM STAFF (LEFT TO RIGHT): BOB PAISLEY, ASSISTANT MANAGER; JOE FAGAN, 1ST TEAM TRAINER; RON MORAN, 2ND TEAM TRAINER; REUBEN BENNETT, SPECIAL DUTIES; AND TOM SAUNDERS, YOUTH TRAINER; PICTURED AT MELWOOD - 8 JULY 1971.

LIVERPOOL'S TREBLE IN 1984

Joe Fagan's wonderful treble

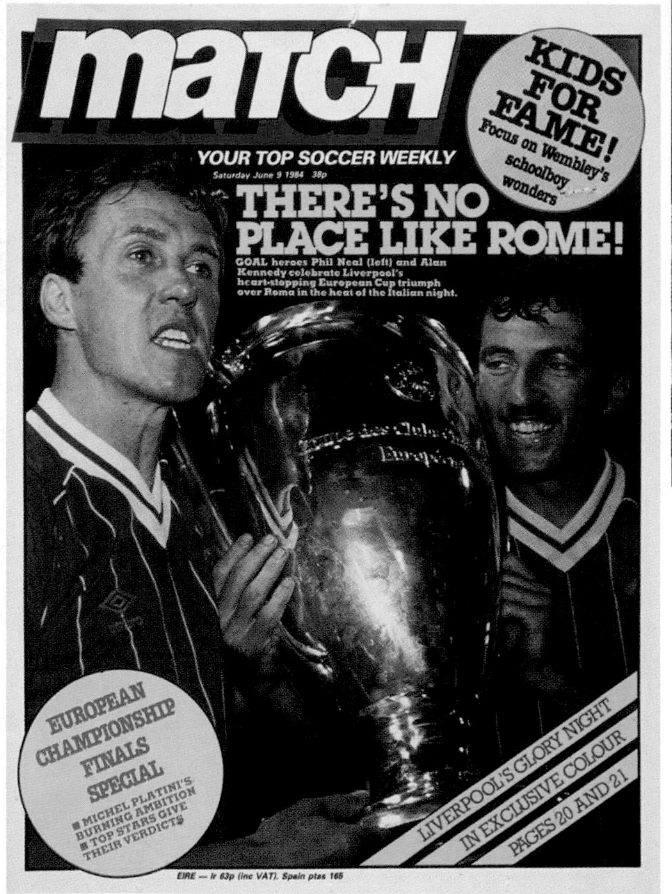
match
KIDS FOR FAME! Focus on Wembley's schoolboy wonders
YOUR TOP SOCCER WEEKLY
Saturday June 9 1984 38p
THERE'S NO PLACE LIKE ROME!
GOAL heroes Phil Neal (left) and Alan Kennedy celebrate Liverpool's heart-stopping European Cup triumph over Roma in the heat of the Italian night.
EUROPEAN CHAMPIONSHIP FINALS SPECIAL
■ MICHEL PLATINI'S BURNING AMBITION
■ TOP STARS GIVE THEIR VERDICTS
LIVERPOOL'S GLORY NIGHT IN EXCLUSIVE COLOUR PAGES 20 AND 21
EIRE — Ir 63p (inc VAT). Spain ptas 165

The League ('Milk') Cup win came after the first ever Merseyside derby at Wembley ended 0-0. With neither side giving an inch and The Toffees being Liverpool's main rivals at the time, the replay was just as close an encounter. The Reds won 1-0 at a packed Maine Road, thanks to a Graeme Souness volley.

The League campaign was sparked into life by a 6-0 win over Luton Town, with Ian Rush grabbing five goals. *That run included five wins in a row, with Liverpool scoring 15 goals and conceding none.*

The traditional season blip had come at Highfield Road, where The Reds lost 0-4 to Coventry, so it was even sweeter when it was a 5-0 win over Coventry which all but won The Reds their 15th Championship. *Ian Rush* bagged four goals in the game and skipper *Alan Hansen* got the other.

Cometh the hour, cometh *Alan Kennedy.* Winning European Cups single-handedly was 'Barney Rubble's' speciality. This time he scored the decisive spot-kick as Liverpool beat AS Roma in their home stadium on penalties with some additional help from *Bruce Grobbelaar's* wobbly leg routine. *It was Liverpool's fourth European Cup win and an incredible end to the season for Joe Fagan especially.*

GRAEME SOUNESS

Liverpool's tough-tackling super Scot

GRAEME SOUNESS STARRED IN THE LIVERPOOL SIDES OF THE LATE 70s AND EARLY 80s AND AS CAPTAIN LIFTED MANY OF THE TROPHIES THE REDS WON.

A tough-tackling central midfielder, he was a leader in every sense. He made sure he imposed himself on the opposition, made vital passes and scored some crucial goals.

Bought from Middlesbrough in January 1978, he had to replace veteran midfielder Ian Callaghan. Although he was a completely different kind of player, Souness quickly won the fans over.

He made his debut in a 1-0 away win over West Brom and scored his first goal, a brilliant volley against Manchester United at Anfield a few weeks later. At the end of that season his slide-rule pass would allow Kenny Dalglish to score the winner against Brugge in the European Cup final.

When Liverpool won the European Cup in 1981 he scored a hat-trick in the quarter-finals against CSKA Sofia. By that time he had also wrested the captaincy from Phil Thompson.

He left for Sampdoria in 1984 with 358 games and 56 goals under his belt for The Reds. *He'd won five Championship medals as well as three European Cups and three League Cups.*

He returned to Anfield as manager in 1991, after a hugely successful spell as player-manager at Rangers. He won the FA Cup with The Reds in 1992, despite being unable to lead the team out at Wembley due to recent heart surgery.

Souness won 54 caps for Scotland and after Liverpool managed Galatasaray, Southampton, Torino, Benfica, Blackburn Rovers and Newcastle United.

"A tough-tackling central midfielder."

HEYSEL AND HILLSBOROUGH

Liverpool's darkest hours

LIVERPOOL'S FIFTH APPEARANCE IN THE EUROPEAN CUP FINAL IN MAY 1985 SHOULD HAVE BEEN A NIGHT OF CELEBRATION. INSTEAD, IT TURNED INTO ONE OF EUROPEAN FOOTBALL'S WORST TRAGEDIES, ESPECIALLY FOR JUVENTUS FOOTBALL CLUB.

The Heysel Stadium, a rundown athletics venue in Brussels, was a terrible choice for the final. To make matters worse Liverpool and Juventus fans were placed next to each other in a tense atmosphere accentuated by the over-zealous Belgian police. After missiles were thrown by both sets of supporters, there was a surge of fans that led to a wall collapsing and 38 Italians and one Belgian supporter lost their lives.

The match was played with Juventus winning 1-0, but no-one cared. *Fourteen Liverpool fans were convicted of manslaughter and English teams were banned from Europe for five years (Liverpool for six).*

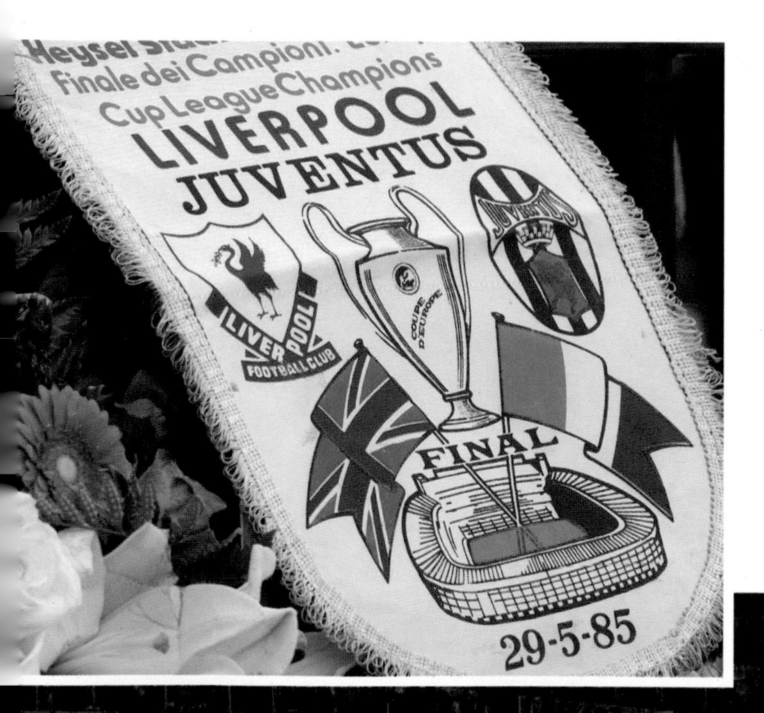

Five years later, an even bigger tragedy at Hillsborough would rob 96 Liverpool supporters of their lives, after poor policing led to a crush at the 1989 FA Cup semi-final.

The original verdict of 'accidental death' was quashed in 2012. Up to that point, most people believed drunken fans had been mostly responsible for the disaster. At the time of writing, the new inquests into the deaths of the 96 are still on-going.

Hillsborough created an even bigger bond between the club and its supporters. The 96 fans who simply went to watch a football match and never came back will never be forgotten. The number 96 is still worn on the back of the players' shirts.

KENNY DALGLISH

The one and only King of The Kop

ALREADY AN IDOL AT CELTIC, LIVERPOOL HAD TO A PAY A RECORD FEE OF £440,000 TO BRING KENNY DALGLISH TO ANFIELD.

It was undoubtedly one of the best pieces of business the club ever did as he became, for many, Liverpool's greatest ever player and also a hugely successful manager.

"He took over as player-manager of The Reds in 1985 and won himself three more League titles and two FA Cups."

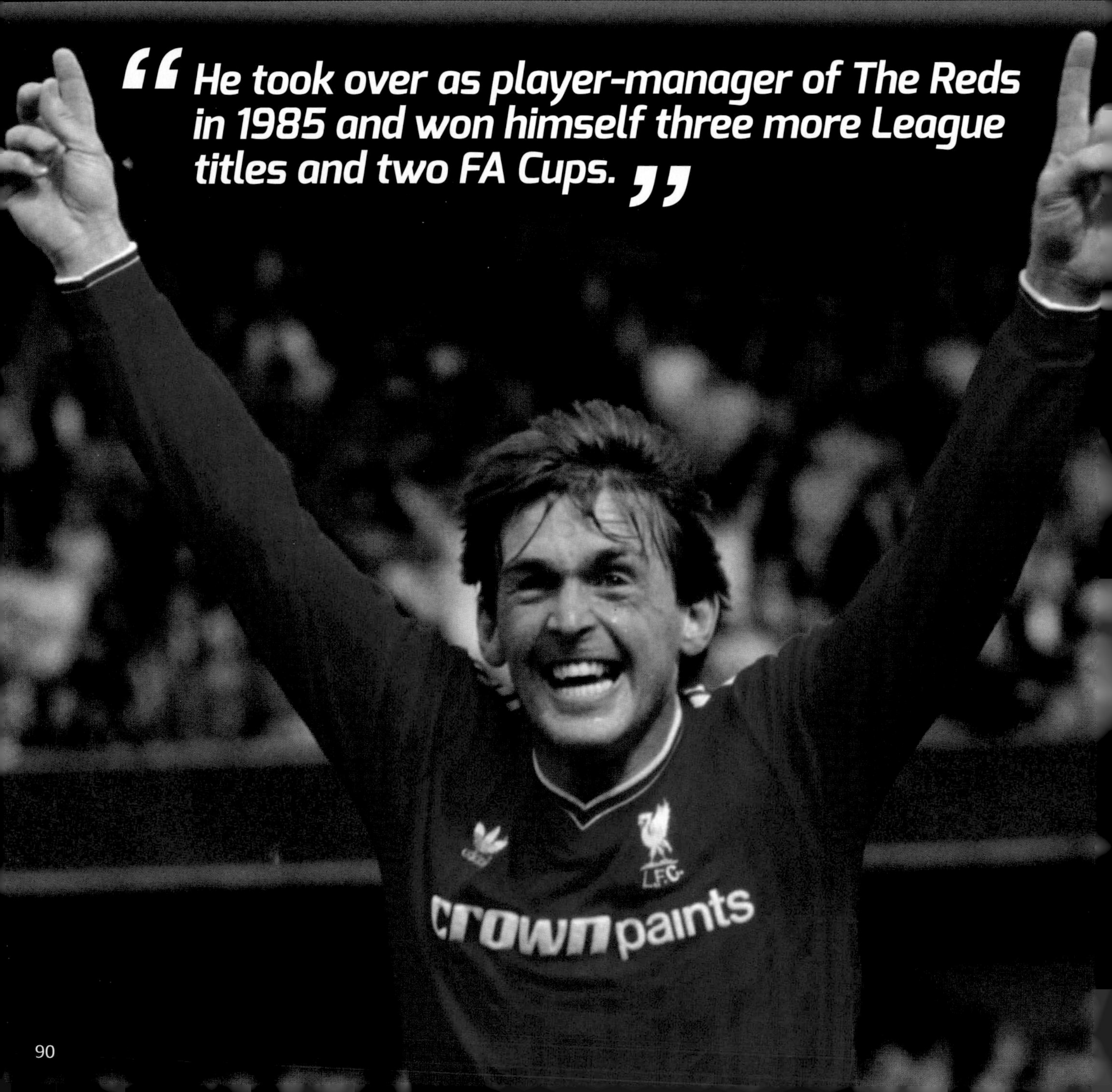

crown paints

RELATIVELY SHORT, BUT STOCKY AND TOUGH, DALGLISH WAS A SKILFUL, SELFLESS PLAYER WITH INCREDIBLE VISION, MATCHED BY FEW PLAYERS THEN OR SINCE. HE WAS ALSO A REGULAR SCORER, AN INCISIVE PASSER AND AS HE LATER PROVED, A SUPERB MOTIVATOR.

He scored within seven minutes of his debut at Middlesbrough in 1978 and then scored again on his home debut in front of The Kop. He sealed his position as the new King of The Kop with his winner in the European Cup final at Wembley at the end of that season.

His medal tally as a player included six League titles, two FA Cups and three European Cups. He is also Scotland's most-capped player with 30 goals from 102 games.

He took over as player-manager of The Reds in 1985 and won himself three more League titles and two FA Cups. Upon leaving the club to steer new club Blackburn Rovers to a Premier League title, he had played 355 games and scored 118 goals.

Dalglish returned for a brief spell as manager of The Reds in 2011 and added yet another League Cup to the Anfield trophy cabinet.

LIVERPOOL PLAYERS KEVIN MCDONALD AND BRUCE GROBBELAAR HOLD THE FA CUP TROPHY ABOVE KENNY DALGLISH AS THEY CELEBRATE ON THEIR LAP OF HONOUR 1986 FA CUP FINAL.

1986 – LIVERPOOL WIN THE CLASSIC DOUBLE

Kenny's reign begins in style

LIVERPOOL CELEBRATE WINNING THE FA CUP 1986.

LIVERPOOL KICKED OFF THE 1985-86 SEASON WITH THE AWFUL CLOUD OF THE HEYSEL DISASTER AND A EUROPEAN BAN HANGING OVER THEM.

Kenny Dalglish had taken over the reins as player-manager and he immediately led the club to an impressive, classic English League and FA Cup double.

This was the era of Merseyside dominance in English football, and it was Everton whom Liverpool had to get the better of to win both League and Cup. The two clubs traded away losses in the derby matches with Liverpool winning 3-2 at Goodison and The Toffees triumphing 2-0 at Anfield.

Ian Rush was the main weapon for The Reds yet again, netting 33 goals for the season, while *Jan Molby* also added an impressive 21 from midfield.

From mid-March to the end of the season, Liverpool only conceded one goal in ten games. That run included a 6-0 win over Oxford and 5-0 wins over Coventry and Birmingham.

The Reds eventually won their 16th title two points ahead of The Toffees. Another famous Dalglish goal led to the deciding win over Chelsea at Stamford Bridge on the last day.

A week later in the FA Cup final at Wembley, Everton initially had Dalglish's team on the rack. They deservedly led at half-time through *Gary Lineker* but second half goals from Rush and *Craig Johnston* won Liverpool the cup.

IAN RUSH

Liverpool's greatest No.9

IAN RUSH WAS QUITE SIMPLY A GOAL MACHINE, A DEADLY ACCURATE FINISHER AND LIVERPOOL'S ALL-TIME TOP SCORER.

The skinny, lithe, moustachioed Welshman was one of the key reasons for Liverpool's dominance of English football in the 1980s. 'Rushie' loved playing against Everton in particular, and ended up with an incredible 25 goals against The Toffees.

"He finished his Liverpool career with 346 goals from 660 games."

Signed from Chester City in 1980, he nearly left after his first season as he felt he wasn't getting enough games under Bob Paisley.

However, in 1981-82, in just his second season, he scored 30 goals. In 1983-84 he scored 47, including hat-tricks against Aston Villa and Benfica, four against Coventry and five against Luton.

In 1986 he left Liverpool for a two-year stint in Italy with Juventus, where although considered something of a failure, he still scored eight goals in a season when 14 was the highest number scored in Serie A. In 1988, just before leaving Juventus, he scored the only goal for Wales in a shock 1-0 win over Italy.

Upon returning to Liverpool in 1988, Rush scored another 90 goals in 245 games with more crucial winners among them. He finished his Liverpool career with 346 goals from 660 games and is still Wales' all-time top scorer with 28.

He is the second highest FA Cup scorer of all time with 44, the record scorer in FA Cup finals with five and the joint record League Cup goalscorer (49) with Geoff Hurst.

LIVERPOOL WIN FIRST DIVISION IN 1988

Dalglish steers Liverpool to 17th title

IN 1988 LIVERPOOL WON THEIR 17TH TITLE AT A CANTER. KENNY DALGLISH'S EXCITING TEAM FINISHED THE SEASON NINE POINTS CLEAR OF RUNNERS-UP MANCHESTER UNITED AND 17 POINTS AHEAD OF THE TEAM IN THIRD, NOTTINGHAM FOREST.

John Barnes, Peter Beardsley and *John Aldridge* starred in a side that put together a 29-game unbeaten run in the league. It started with a 2-1 win over Arsenal at Highbury on the opening day and lasted until they lost 0-1 at Everton in the derby in March.

They also scored four or more 11 times and had a ten-game run where they didn't concede a goal. Barnes and Beardsley netted 30 goals between them, while *Steve Nicol* scored six from full-back.

> **"It was the finest exhibition I've seen in the whole time I've watched the game."**
>
> **- Sir Tom Finney**

A fortnight after the derby they lost 1-2 to title rivals Forest at the City Ground. However, *The Reds soon reasserted themselves and wreaked a perfect revenge over Brian Clough's talented young side.* Just a week later they beat Forest in the FA Cup semi-final and then beat them 5-0 in one of the most one-sided games ever seen in the First Division.

It was a demolition of one of the top sides in the country at that time and prompted none other than Sir Tom Finney to declare: "It was the finest exhibition I've seen in the whole time I've watched the game".

The title was clinched two games later with four games to go, by a 1-0 win over Spurs at Anfield courtesy of a first half Peter Beardsley goal.

LIVERPOOL WIN THE FA CUP IN 1989

Cup win overshadowed by the 96 lives lost at Hillsborough

IN 1989 LIVERPOOL WON THE FA CUP FOR THE FOURTH TIME, AGAIN OVER EVERTON, AND AGAIN WITH TWO GOALS FROM IAN RUSH, WHO CAME OFF THE BENCH TO SEAL THE 3-2 WIN.

"The final the country wanted."

- The Daily Mirror

HOWEVER, THE EVENT WAS OVERSHADOWED BY THE HILLSBOROUGH TRAGEDY JUST FIVE WEEKS EARLIER. The 95 (later 96) fans who died were rightly on the minds of everybody at Wembley that day.

The 1988-89 FA Cup run was the first time Liverpool had got to the final without needing any replays.

They started the campaign with three away ties, all against lower league opposition. Carlisle were beaten 3-0, then a Millwall side featuring future Red *Jimmy Carter* and *Teddy Sheringham* were seen off 2-0.

Hull City were beaten 3-2 in the fifth round and Brentford 4-0 in the quarter-finals, in Liverpool's only FA Cup game that season at Anfield.

After the horror of Hillsborough, Liverpool beat Nottingham Forest 3-1 at Old Trafford to set up what the Daily Mirror called "the final the country wanted".

That final saw Liverpool hanging on for victory after a fourth minute goal from John Aldridge. However, substitute Stuart McCall equalised for Everton in the 89th minute to send the game into extra-time. He also equalised again for The Toffees after Rush, *Liverpool's own super sub, put them ahead again in the 94th minute.*

But it was Rush who was to make history as he scored another Wembley double to win The Reds the Cup.

CENTENARY PICTURE OF LIVERPOOL TEAM, PHOTOCALL AT ANFIELD TO CELEBRATE THE 100 YEAR ANNIVERSARY OF THE FOOTBALL CLUB WHICH WAS FORMED IN 1892. PICTURE TAKEN IN JULY 1992.

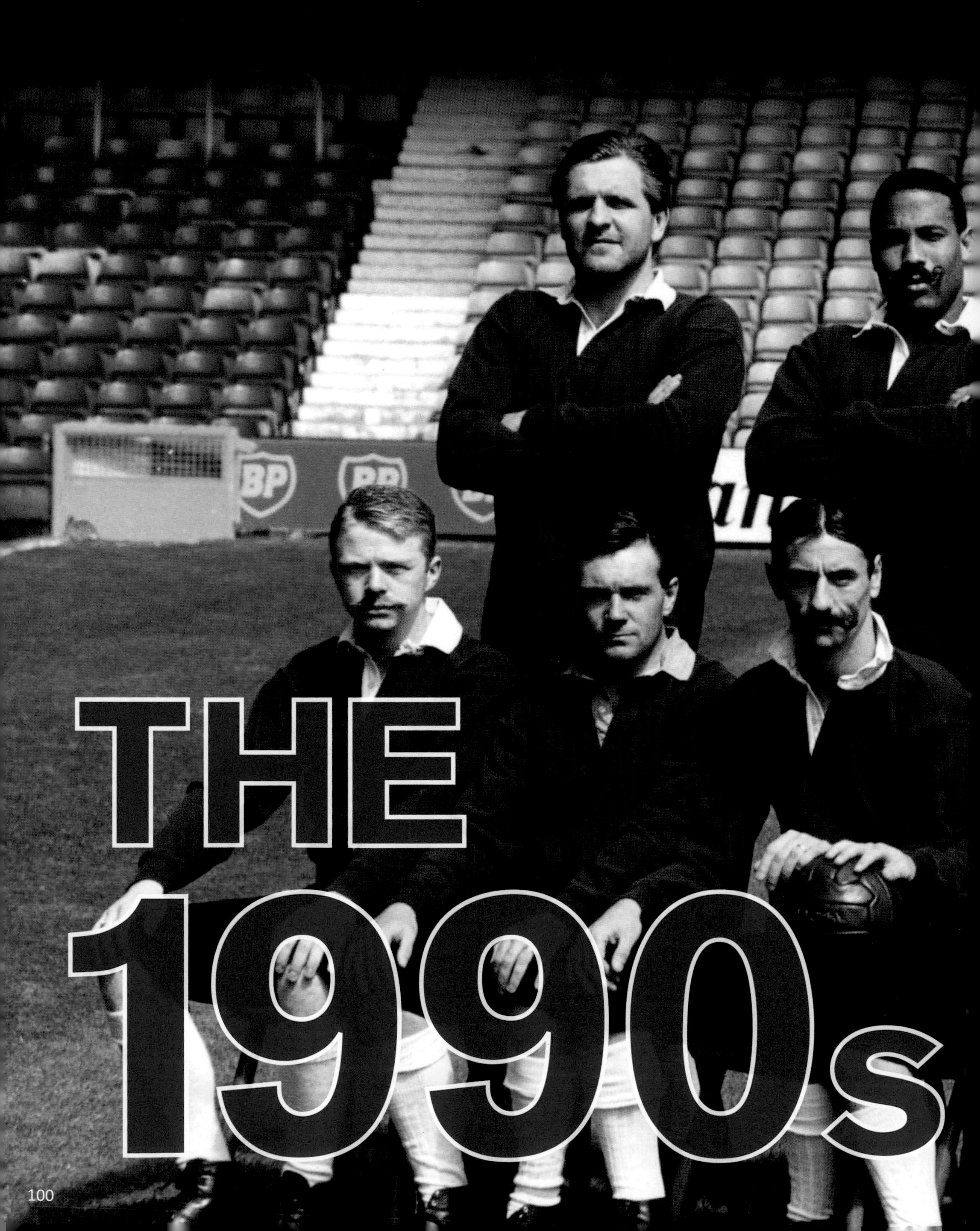

THE 1990s

Back Row left to right: Jan Molby, John Barnes, Bruce Grobbelaar, Steve Nicol and Mark Wright. Front row left to right: David Burrows, Ray Houghton, Ian Rush, Dean Saunders, Rob Jones and Ronnie Whelan.

LIVERPOOL BEGAN THE 1990S WITH THEIR 18TH LEAGUE TITLE, BUT LITTLE DID THEY KNOW THAT IT WAS TO BE THEIR LAST TO DATE AND THAT OVER THE NEXT 25 YEARS, TROPHIES WOULD BECOME A MORE HARD TO COME BY COMMODITY AT ANFIELD.

The 1989-90 season saw John Aldridge leave for Real Sociedad. His last game was a stunning 9-0 win over Crystal Palace. The Londoners would have the last laugh, however, by knocking The Reds out of the FA Cup 3-4 in an amazing semi-final encounter.

John Barnes weighed in with 28 goals and a Footballer of the Year award to temper Aldridge's loss, as Liverpool finished nine points clear of Aston Villa.

By February 1991 things were looking rosy again for The Reds as they battled for the title with Arsenal. However, four matches against Everton (with a 1-3 loss to Luton Town sandwiched in between) changed all that.

Liverpool won the derby at Anfield 3-1 on the 9th then drew 0-0 at home in the fifth round of the FA Cup on the 17th. The replay on February 20th was an amazing 4-4 draw at Goodison which precipitated manager Kenny Dalglish's resignation.

Caretaker boss Ronnie Moran had to deal with the loss at Luton and then with his team going out to The Toffees in the cup, as they won the second replay at Goodison 1-0.

SEASON	DIVISION	P	W	D	L	F	A	D	POS
1990-91	Division 1	38	23	7	8	77	40	76	2nd
1991-92	Division 1	42	16	16	10	47	40	64	6th
1992-93	PL	42	16	11	15	62	55	59	6th
1993-94	PL	42	17	9	16	59	55	60	8th
1994-95	PL	42	21	11	10	65	37	74	4th

However, The Reds eventually rallied in the league, beating Derby 7-1 and Leeds 5-4, just before Graeme Souness was appointed manager in April.

A 2-4 home defeat to Chelsea, however, handed Arsenal the title with The Reds eventually finishing seven points behind them.

In 1992 Souness led his team to a fifth FA Cup victory. They beat Sunderland 2-0 at Wembley with goals from Michael Thomas and record-breaker Ian Rush. However, Liverpool's league form was poor and two consecutive 6th place finishes saw Souness resign.

Boot Room graduate Roy Evans took over in January 1994 and despite a League Cup win in 1995, he couldn't improve The Reds' league form either.

By July 1998 he had been joined in a joint-manager experiment by Frenchman Gerard Houllier but it didn't work, and Evans resigned in November after 35 years employment with the club.

Liverpool's most successful manager, Bob Paisley, had passed away in 1996 and the club paid tribute to him by opening 'The Paisley Gateway' in 1999 in a fitting end to the decade.

SEASON	DIVISION	P	W	D	L	F	A	D	POS
1995-96	PL	38	20	11	7	70	34	71	3rd
1996-97	PL	38	19	11	8	62	37	68	4th
1997-98	PL	38	18	11	9	68	42	65	3rd
1998-99	PL	38	15	9	14	68	49	54	7th
1999-00	PL	38	19	10	9	51	30	67	4th

ALAN HANSEN

Cool and classy, the model central defender

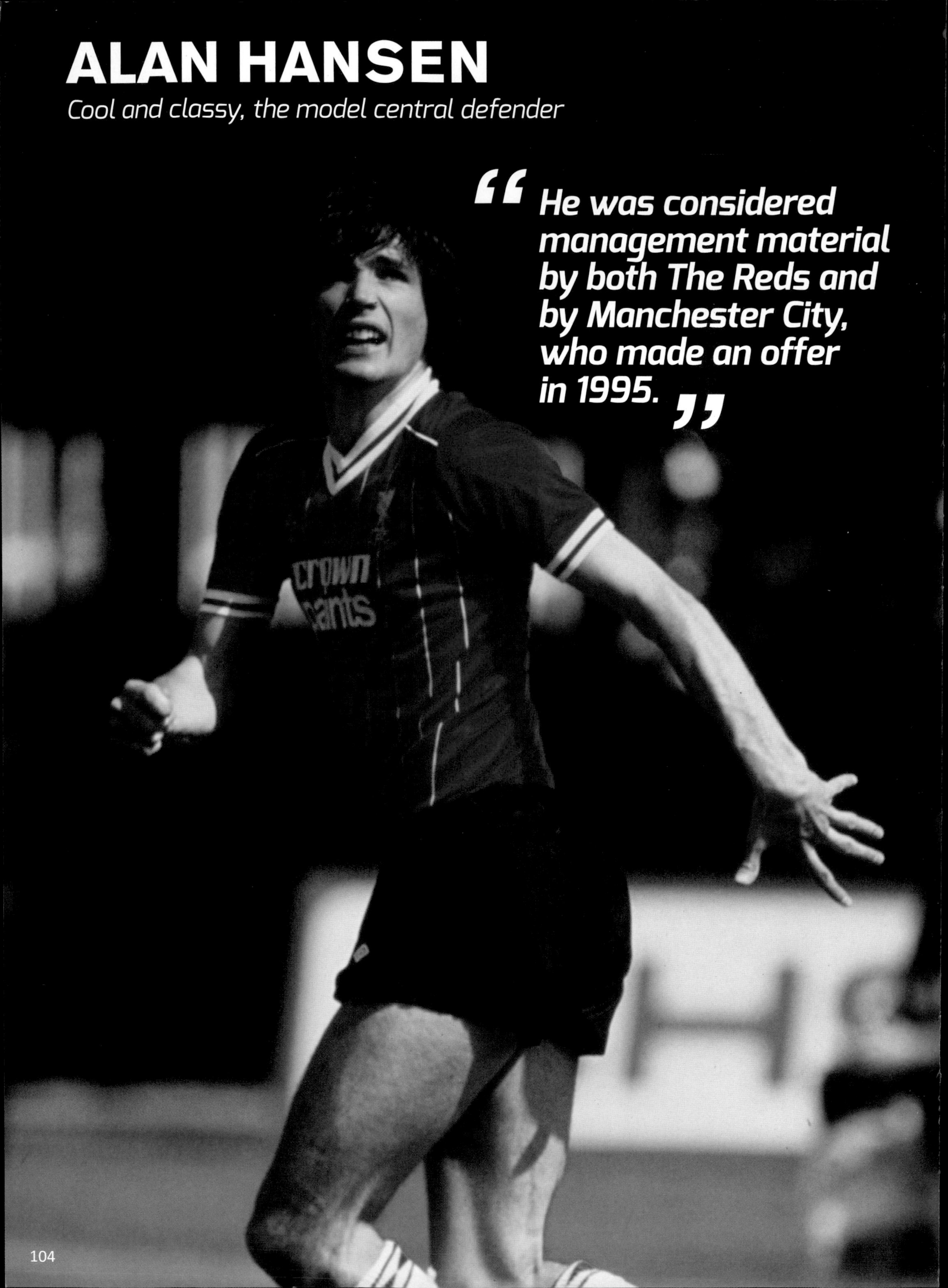

"He was considered management material by both The Reds and by Manchester City, who made an offer in 1995."

ANOTHER IN LIVERPOOL'S LONG LINE OF FAMOUS SCOTS, ALAN HANSEN WAS PROBABLY THE CLASSIEST CENTRE-HALF THE CLUB EVER HAD.

He was signed from Partick Thistle in 1977 after playing 86 games for them over four seasons. He had watched his brother John play in the Thistle side that shocked Celtic by beating them 4-1 in the 1971 Scottish League Cup final.

Always calm under pressure and with an acute sense of timing in the tackle, Hansen's 13 years at the heart of The Reds defence brought him a huge haul of medals. *He won eight league titles, three European Cups and an FA Cup, captaining Liverpool to the double in 1989.*

As well as being a professional-level golfer, Hansen was a talented basketball, volleyball, and squash player in his youth. But he was only capped 26 times for Scotland and was bafflingly left out of their 1986 World Cup squad by Alex Ferguson. He made his international debut in a 3-0 defeat to Wales in which John Toshack grabbed a hat-trick.

Hansen stayed at Liverpool until the end of his career in 1991. *He notched up 434 games, scoring eight goals.* He was considered management material by both The Reds and by Manchester City, who made an offer in 1995.

But he was never interested in coaching or management, saying in The Guardian "I was never tempted, I wanted to keep my hair relatively black". Hansen became a popular TV pundit on Match of the Day instead.

LIVERPOOL V QUEENS PARK RANGERS - ANFIELD - 28 APRIL 1990 - LIVERPOOL PLAYERS ACKNOWLEDGE THEIR FANS AND CELEBRATE WINNING THE LEAGUE CHAMPIONSHIP (L-R) JOHN BARNES, DAVID BURROWS, GARY GILLESPIE, BARRY VENISON, JAN MOLBY, RAY HOUGHTON, IAN RUSH, GLEN HYSEN AND BRUCE GROBBELAAR.

LIVERPOOL WIN FIRST DIVISION IN 1990

Reds' 18th title triumph

FA CUP SEMI FINAL - CRYSTAL PALACE V LIVERPOOL - 8 APRIL 1990 - IAN RUSH SHOOTS PAST NIGEL MARTYN TO SCORE.

LIVERPOOL WON THEIR 18TH TITLE IN 1990, IN A SEASON WHICH SAW JOHN ALDRIDGE LEAVE FOR REAL SOCIEDAD. HOWEVER, JOHN BARNES WEIGHED IN WITH 28 GOALS AND ADDED A WELL-DESERVED FOOTBALLER OF THE YEAR AWARD TO HIS HONOURS.

The Reds got the season off to a flier, beating Manchester City 3-1 at home on the first day, and went on to score 27 goals in the next nine games.

As has been the case since, Liverpool's relationship with Crystal Palace was an interesting one that season. On the wrong end of a 9-0 hammering at Anfield, the South London outfit beat The Reds 3-4 in one of the best and most dramatic FA Cup semi-finals ever.

> *"One of the best and most dramatic FA Cup semi-finals ever."*

With that defeat hanging over them, the end of the season approached and Liverpool were locked in a three-way title race with Arsenal and Aston Villa. Next up was a tricky game with Charlton Athletic, who were desperate for points to avoid relegation.

An unlikely saviour stepped forward in the shape of striker *Ronny Rosenthal*. The Israeli centre-forward scored a hat-trick on his full debut in the Charlton game, giving The Reds the impetus to go on and win the league for the 18th time.

In the end a 2-1 victory over Queens Park Rangers was enough for them to be crowned champions with two games to spare. Villa were left trailing by nine points in second and Arsenal finished fourth, after Spurs leapfrogged them on the last day.

STEVE NICOL

Unsung hero under three managers

STEVE NICOL WAS A BARGAIN BUY FOR THE REDS FOR JUST £300,000 FROM AYR UNITED.

He joined in 1981, making his debut under Bob Paisley in a 0-0 draw against Birmingham City in 1982. He had to wait until the 1983-84 season to become a regular under Joe Fagan, *winning a League Championship winner's medal and netting his first goal,* the only goal of the game in a 1-0 win over QPR.

He earned the strange nickname 'Chopsy' among his team-mates for the way he pronounced the word 'chips', but he was highly regarded for his versatility and skill.

> ***"In all he won five League Championships, three FA Cups and a European Cup."***

Nicol played mostly at right-back but was equally comfortable at left-back, and could play centre-back or in midfield. He made his international debut for Scotland in 1986 and was in the squad for the World Cup that year in Mexico.

He was in phenomenal form in 1987-88, scoring a memorable hat-trick from full-back against Newcastle and a stunning long-range header against Arsenal at Highbury.

He was just as reliable the next season, when he picked up the Football Writers' Association Footballer of the Year Award. In all he won five League Championships, three FA Cups and a European Cup in a 13-year, 468-game career with The Reds. He also scored 46 goals, a remarkable return for a full-back.

He went on to play for Notts County and Sheffield Wednesday and had a successful spell as manager of New England Revolution in the USA.

LIVERPOOL WIN THE FA CUP IN 1992

Reds beat Sunderland 2-0 to claim fifth FA Cup

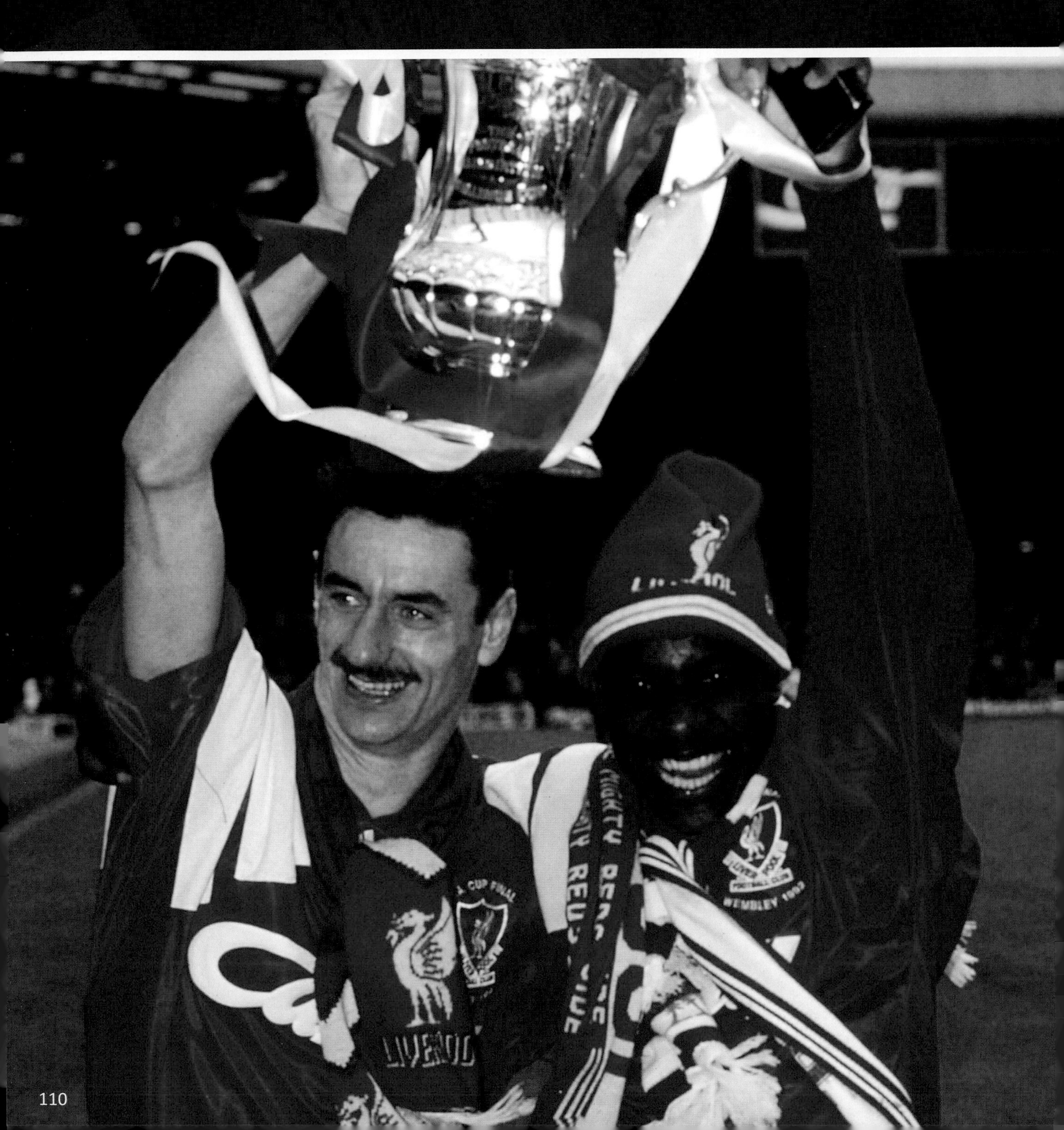

LIVERPOOL WON THEIR FIFTH FA CUP IN 1992, ON A DAY WHICH BELONGED TO LEGENDARY STRIKER IAN RUSH, PLAYING AND SCORING IN HIS THIRD AND LAST FINAL.

Rush broke the record for the most goals in FA Cup finals when he notched the second in a 2-0 win over Sunderland. It was his fifth in finals overall.

John Barnes grabbed a hat-trick as Crewe Alexandra were dispatched 4-0 in the third round, though Liverpool then needed replays to beat Bristol Rovers and Ipswich Town in rounds four and five. A solo *Michael Thomas* effort was enough to end Aston Villa's challenge in the quarter-final.

In the semi-final a resolute and skilful Portsmouth team stood in their way. 120 minutes of football failed to separate the two sides, but a penalty shoot-out sent The Reds through.

Recent heart surgery meant manager *Graeme Souness* was at pitch-side but was not deemed fit enough to lead the team out at Wembley. Instead, the honour fell to Boot Room stalwart and unanimous choice, *Ronnie Moran*, who had missed out as a player when Liverpool won the cup in 1965.

Thomas gave Liverpool the lead with a brilliant strike just after half-time and that man Rush then sealed it for the Red men with his record-breaking goal in the 67th minute.

Skipper *Mark Wright* led the team up the famous Wembley steps to lift his only major trophy in 210 games for the club.

JOHN BARNES

Liverpool's enthralling left-wing wizard

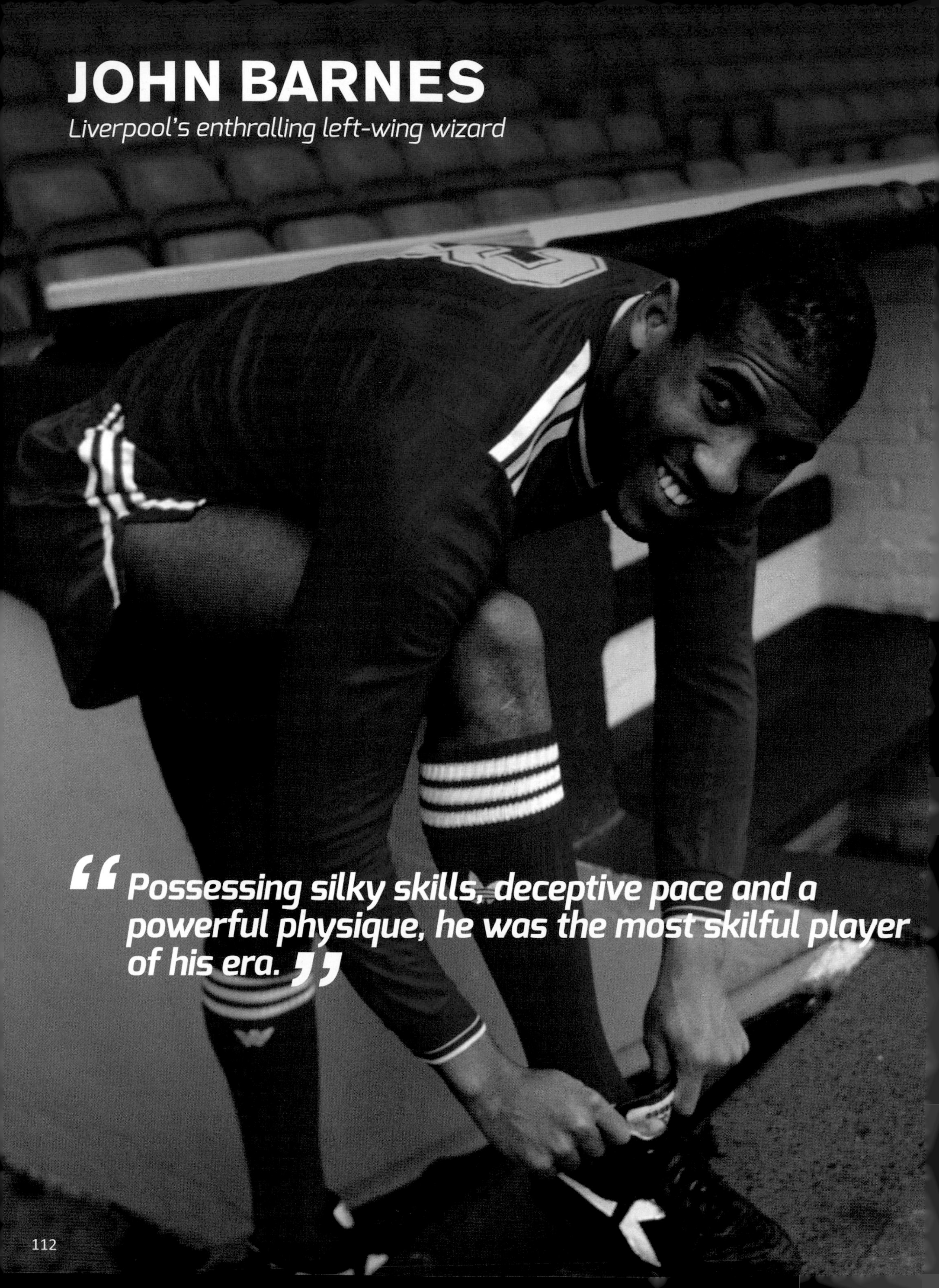

> **"Possessing silky skills, deceptive pace and a powerful physique, he was the most skilful player of his era."**

BORN INTO A MILITARY FAMILY IN KINGSTON, JAMAICA, AND NAMED AFTER WELSH FOOTBALLER JOHN CHARLES, JOHN BARNES MOVED TO LONDON WHEN HE WAS 12.

He initially played for Watford, and with 233 appearances and 65 goals, was a key figure in the club's most successful period.

Possessing silky skills, deceptive pace and a powerful physique, he was the most skilful player of his era and in 2007, *Four Four Two magazine voted him the best player of all time.*

Signed by Kenny Dalglish in 1987 after being turned down by Alex Ferguson in favour of Jesper Olsen, Barnes formed a formidable Reds attacking midfield partnership with Peter Beardsley.

Practically his first kick of a ball for the club saw him combine with Beardsley to set up John Aldridge for a goal. It was in the 9th minute of a 2-1 win over Arsenal on the first day of the 1987-88 season.

In ten years with The Reds, Barnes won two First Division titles and two FA Cups, and was also named PFA Player of the Year twice.

Although considered something of an enigma on the international stage, he played 79 times for England, *and among his 11 goals was a famous solo effort against Brazil in the Maracana.*

Barnes left Anfield for Newcastle United in 1997 and also played a few games for Charlton Athletic. His career in management never really took off and his jobs with Celtic, Jamaica and Tranmere Rovers were all short-lived.

LIVERPOOL WIN THE LEAGUE CUP IN 1995

McManaman the main man as Reds break another record

THE LEAGUE CUP FINAL OF 1995 WAS LIVERPOOL'S 30TH APPEARANCE AT WEMBLEY AND SAW THEM WIN THE TROPHY FOR A RECORD FIFTH TIME.

The star of the show was local-born midfielder Steve McManaman, who scored both Liverpool goals in a 2-1 win over Bruce Rioch's Bolton Wanderers. It was sweet revenge for The Reds after The Trotters had knocked them out of the FA Cup the season before.

Robbie Fowler had announced his presence in audacious fashion in the same competition the previous year, scoring all five goals in a second round 5-0 win over Fulham at Anfield.

This time around he beat Crystal Palace single-handedly, though not quite as dramatically. The young centre-forward scored both winners as Liverpool won 1-0 at Anfield and Selhurst Park, to set up the final against Wanderers.

But it was his fellow Scouser who lit up Wembley. A classic, dribbling winger, *McManaman* had only scored once in five months before the big game, but was clearly saving his best for Wembley. Both goals were superb and rightly earned him the Man of the Match award.

Although *Alan Thompson* scored just after McManaman's second, *Liverpool were on top and comfortably held on to win.*

Fittingly, it was *Ian Rush* who led the team up the Wembley steps, holding the trophy aloft as captain for the first and last time in his incredible Liverpool career.

THE 2000s

THOUSANDS OF SUPPORTERS CELEBRATE AS LIVERPOOL PASS THROUGH ST. JOHN'S GARDENS IN THE CENTRE OF LIVERPOOL ON THE OPEN-TOP BUS, MAY 26, 2005.

LIVERPOOL DEFEATED ITALIAN CLUB AC MILAN 3-2 ON PENALTIES IN THE CHAMPIONS LEAGUE FINAL FOLLOWING A DRAMATIC 3-3 DRAW AFTER EXTRA-TIME IN ISTANBUL.

SEASON	DIVISION	P	W	D	L	F	A	D	POS
2000-01	PL	38	20	9	9	71	39	69	3rd
2001-02	PL	38	24	8	6	67	30	80	2nd
2002-03	PL	38	18	10	10	61	41	64	5th
2003-04	PL	38	16	12	10	55	37	60	4th
2004-05	PL	38	17	7	14	52	41	58	5th

LIVERPOOL STARTED THE NEW MILLENNIUM GRADUALLY IMPROVING UNDER GERARD HOULLIER. THEY FINISHED FOURTH IN THE PREMIER LEAGUE IN 2000, THEN THIRD IN 2001 AND WERE RUNNERS-UP TO ARSENAL IN 2002.

Although falling away in the league in 2000-01, Houllier's team still pulled off a marvellous treble. First they secured the League Cup by beating Birmingham City at the Millennium Stadium in Cardiff.

They were back there a few months later for the FA Cup final against Arsenal. The Gunners dominated the match but only managed to score one goal through Freddie Ljungberg, which left the door open for a late Reds surge. Michael Owen scored in the 83rd and 88th minutes to steal the cup from under their noses.

The next stop was the Westfalen Stadium in Dortmund for the UEFA Cup final against Spanish minnows Alaves, who were having the season of their lives. An amazing match ended 4-4 in normal time with Markus Babbel, Steven Gerrard, Gary McAllister and Robbie Fowler netting for The Reds. *The game was settled when the unfortunate Delfi Geli headed into his own net to give Liverpool a golden goal win.*

Three trophies turned into five in the calendar year of 2001 when The Reds also won the Charity Shield and the European Super Cup at the start of the 2001-02 season.

Houllier added a League Cup final win over Manchester United to the trophy cabinet in 2003, but couldn't halt the team's poor form in the league and he was sacked in May 2004.

A month later Rafa Benitez took the reins after joining from Valencia. In his first few months he led Liverpool to a League Cup final, which they lost 3-2 to Chelsea, but things would get significantly better for the Spaniard from thereon in.

Firstly his team got revenge over Jose Mourhino's Chelsea in the Champions League semi-finals, before then they somehow overcame a 0-3 half-time deficit to AC Milan in the final, on what has become known as *'The Greatest Night'* and *'The Miracle of Istanbul'.*

Liverpool won the FA Cup in 2006, with Steven Gerrard in unstoppable form, and reached another Champions League final in 2007. This time, however, AC Milan got revenge for Istanbul, winning 2-1 in Athens.

In Benitez's penultimate season in charge, The Reds finished the season again as Premier League runners-up, but beat Manchester United and Chelsea home and away and also recorded a *5-0 aggregate win over Real Madrid in the Champions League.*

SEASON	DIVISION	P	W	D	L	F	A	D	POS
2005-06	PL	38	25	7	6	57	25	82	3rd
2006-07	PL	38	20	8	10	57	27	68	3rd
2007-08	PL	38	21	13	4	67	28	76	4th
2008-09	PL	38	25	11	2	77	27	86	2nd
2009-10	PL	38	18	9	11	61	35	63	7th

GERARD HOULLIER

From job-sharing to the treble in three years

GERARD HOULLIER'S CAREER AS LIVERPOOL MANAGER BEGAN IN THE UNUSUAL CIRCUMSTANCES OF A SHARED ROLE WITH ROY EVANS IN 1998.

Liverpool clearly felt unable to sack the loyal Boot Room lieutenant Evans. However Houllier, initially brought in to replace Ronnie Moran as No.2 to Evans, was always going to be more than a deputy. The solution of having two managers was certainly different, but doomed to failure, and lasted just four months when Evans resigned.

Before joining The Reds, Houllier had managed Lens, Paris St. Germain and the French national team.

Although not a top player, he played in Liverpool as a student and in the French lower leagues for AC Le Touquet, in his home area of the Pas-de-Calais.

By the 2000-01 season, Houllier's rebuilding of the squad was well underway and, with the likes of Markus Babbel, Gary McAllister and Emile Heskey at their peak, had put together a winning squad.

That season Liverpool won the FA Cup, League Cup and the UEFA Cup. *They also added the Charity Shield and the UEFA Super Cup to give Houllier a haul of five trophies in the calendar year of 2001.*

In October of that year, Houllier was rushed to hospital for heart surgery after falling ill during a game with Leeds. He never really managed to hit the heights of the treble season again and left Liverpool in 2004 for Lyon. He later also had a brief spell in the Premier League with Aston Villa.

"Although not a top player, he played in Liverpool as a student and in the French lower leagues."

ROBBIE FOWLER

God for short

TOXTETH-BORN ROBBIE FOWLER IS THE SIXTH-HIGHEST SCORER IN PREMIER LEAGUE HISTORY AND WAS NICKNAMED 'GOD', SUCH WAS HIS POPULARITY ON THE KOP.

He was an irrepressible character and an instinctive poacher who plundered 183 goals for The Reds, including a fastest-ever Premier League hat-trick.

Fowler was a schoolboy prodigy who once scored 16 times in a game for his junior side Thorvald. He signed as a youth team player for Liverpool in 1991 and became a professional on his 17th birthday, 9 April 1992.

Still only 19, ***Fowler scored on his debut in a 3-1 League Cup win over Fulham at Craven Cottage in 1993*** and then stunned the Anfield faithful by scoring all five in a 5-0 win in the return leg.

His scored his first league goal in his next game against Oldham and then notched his first league hat-trick (in only his fifth league game) against Southampton.

Fowler was ever-present for Liverpool in 1994-95, playing 57 games. His stunning strike should have won Liverpool the first League Cup final to be played in Cardiff, but in the end they had to do it the hard way on penalties.

That season also included his famous four-minute hat-trick against Arsenal, which was a Premier League record for 20 years.

Fowler also scored 20 league goals in three seasons for Manchester City, four for Cardiff City and 14 for Leeds United. He netted seven times for England in 26 games.

LIVERPOOL WIN A NEW TREBLE IN 2001

Houllier's fantastic season

IN AN AMAZING SEASON IN 2000-01, THE REDS PICKED UP THE FA CUP, LEAGUE CUP AND UEFA CUP, THANKS PARTLY TO TWO OF THE DEADLIEST STRIKERS IN THE CLUB'S HISTORY.

Robbie Fowler, *a Kop hero, Scouser and natural goalscorer, had a street footballer's instincts and a knack for scoring vital goals.*

ROBBIE FOWLER (C LEFT) AND SAMI HYYPIA (C RIGHT) LIFT THE UEFA CUP AFTER WINNING THE FINAL AGAINST ALAVES AT DORTMUND'S WESTFALEN STADIUM, 16 MAY 2001. LIVERPOOL WON A THRILLER 5-4 AFTER EXTRA-TIME.

Like Fowler, Michael Owen was another teenage prodigy who scored 158 goals and went on to play for Real Madrid, as well as scoring some key goals for England.

Fowler's stunning strike should have won Liverpool the first League Cup final to be played in Cardiff, but in the end they had to do it the hard way, on penalties.

Liverpool were back in Cardiff a few months later to take on Arsenal in the FA Cup final. *With six minutes to go and trailing a superior Gunners' side 1-0, Owen wrote his name into Kop history with two quick-fire strikes* which turned the game on its head.

Liverpool also won their third UEFA Cup the hard way, beating Spain's Alaves 5-4 in extra-time. Owen played brilliantly, providing an assist and being brought down for a penalty. In the end a cruel own goal won it for The Reds after Fowler had come off the bench to score the fourth.

When they then beat Manchester United in the Charity Shield and Bayern Munich in the UEFA Super Cup at the start of the following season, *It mean Liverpool had won an incredible five trophies in 2001.*

MICHAEL OWEN

Liverpool's pocket-rocket goal poacher extraordinaire

THE SON OF FORMER EVERTON PLAYER TERRY OWEN, MICHAEL OWEN WAS, LIKE ROBBIE FOWLER, A SCHOOLBOY PRODIGY WITH AN INCREDIBLE SCORING RECORD.

At the age of nine he was captain of the Deeside Area Primary Schools Under-11s, and overhauled a record a certain Ian Rush had held for 20 years, scoring 97 goals in a season.

"Lightning-quick with a superb touch, he also had a powerful shot and a lethal eye for goal."

He signed schoolboy terms with Liverpool at the age of 12 and was attending the FA's School of Excellence at Lilleshall two years later, scoring 28 goals in 20 games for England Under-15s and Under-16s.

During the 1995-96 season he scored 11 goals in five matches in Liverpool's first ever FA Youth Cup win.

Lightning-quick with a superb touch, he also had a powerful shot and a lethal eye for goal.

Owen made a goalscoring debut for The Reds in a game against Wimbledon at the end of the 1996-97 season. He then replaced the injured Robbie Fowler as The Reds' centre-forward for 1997-98 and immediately won the Premier League Golden Boot, *netting 18 times and winning the PFA Young Player of the Year award.*

He won the Golden Boot again the following season, again scoring 18 goals. *He helped The Reds to Gerard Houllier's famous treble in 2001,* winning the FA Cup final single-handedly against Arsenal and scoring in the UEFA Cup final win.

Owen left Liverpool for Real Madrid in 2004.

LIVERPOOL WIN THE LEAGUE CUP IN 2003

Houllier grabs his second League Cup

BACK IN THE MILLENNIUM STADIUM IN 2003 FOR A THIRD FINAL THERE, LIVERPOOL WON THEIR SEVENTH LEAGUE CUP WITH A 2-0 WIN OVER THE OLD ENEMY MANCHESTER UNITED.

In the semi-final, first leg at Bramall Lane, Neil Mellor had given The Reds a first-half lead but two late goals from Sheffield United's Michael Tonge handed the Yorkshiremen a slender 2-1 advantage to take to Anfield.

In the second leg, *El Hadji Diouf* scored early on before *Michael Owen* made it 2-0 in extra-time to send The Reds to Cardiff 3-2 on aggregate.

In the final, a star-studded United side included the likes of Ruud Van Nistelrooy, Ryan Giggs and David Beckham, but they couldn't break down a Reds defence marshalled by the giant Finn *Sami Hyypia*.

The clean sheet kept by goalkeeper *Jerzy Dudek* was well earned, with some spectacular saves keeping out United's forwards. However, the likeable Pole's greatest night as Liverpool's No.1 was still to come.

Steven Gerrard tried his luck on 38 minutes and gave Liverpool the lead when his powerful shot deflected off Beckham and over Fabien Barthez. United should have levelled a number of times but with Dudek in the form of his life and *Stephane Henchoz* clearing off the line, they simply couldn't find a way through.

With four minutes left, *Michael Owen* sent the travelling Kop into raptures, making the final score 2-0 and giving *Gerard Houllier* his sixth trophy in three years.

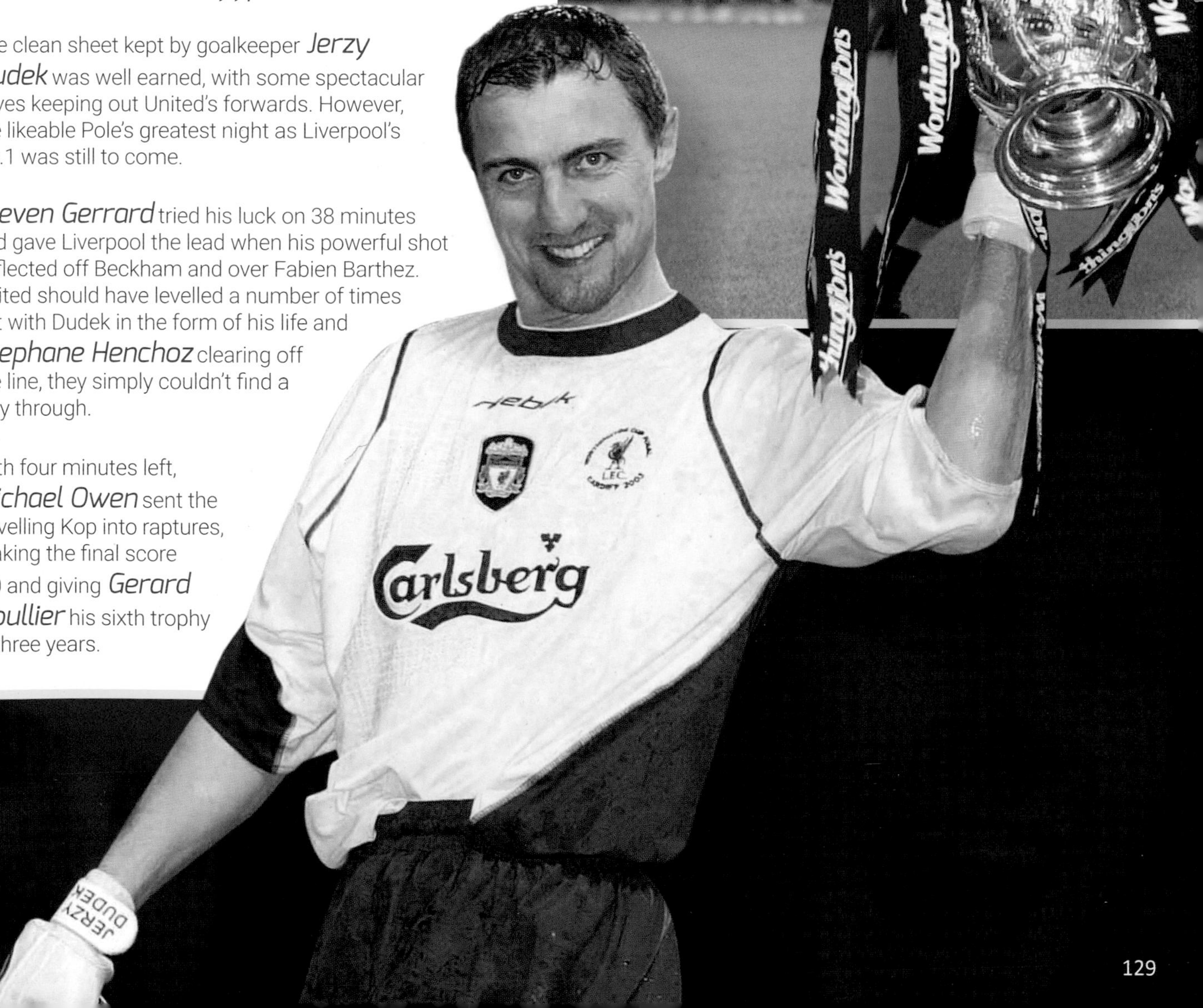

SPOTLIGHT ON: THE LEAGUE CUP

The trophy The Reds have made their own

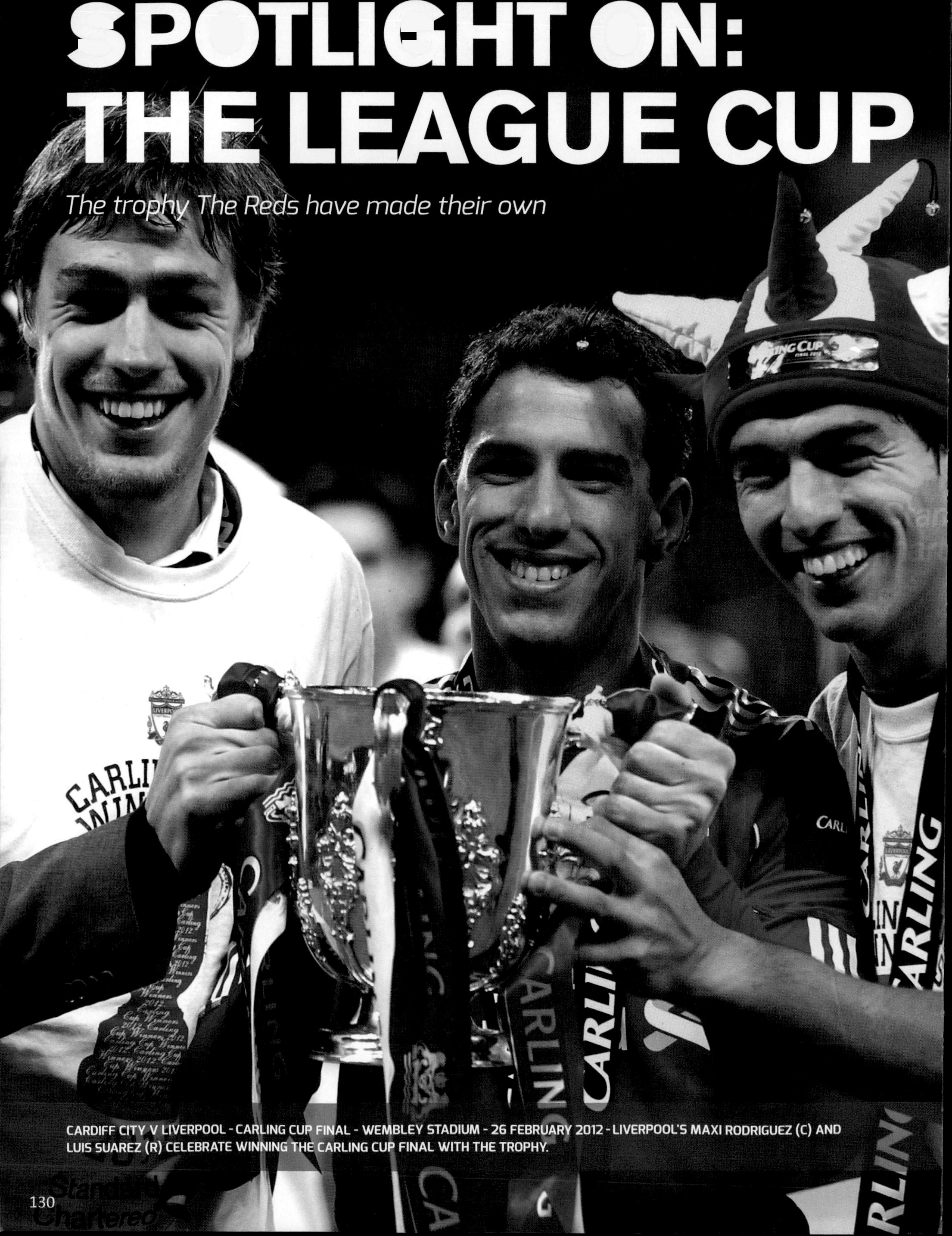

CARDIFF CITY V LIVERPOOL - CARLING CUP FINAL - WEMBLEY STADIUM - 26 FEBRUARY 2012 - LIVERPOOL'S MAXI RODRIGUEZ (C) AND LUIS SUAREZ (R) CELEBRATE WINNING THE CARLING CUP FINAL WITH THE TROPHY.

IT TOOK LIVERPOOL UNTIL 1981 TO WIN THE LEAGUE CUP FOR THE FIRST TIME, BUT THEY WENT ON TO WIN IT ANOTHER SEVEN TIMES.

At the time of writing they have a record eight wins from 11 finals, ahead of Aston Villa and Chelsea both on five.

Ian Rush has the most winners' medals as a player with five, and also jointly holds the record for the most League Cup final appearances with Emile Heskey on six. Heskey played two finals for The Reds, plus three for Leicester City and one for Aston Villa.

Rush is also joint-record scorer in the competition, on 49 with Geoff Hurst.

Liverpool jointly hold the record for the biggest win with West Ham. In 1986 The Reds beat Fulham 10-0, and The Hammers' win over Bury in 1983.

The Reds also hold one of the more unusual records in the competition with the most penalties in a shoot-out. Brendan Rodgers' team finally edged out Middlesbrough 14-13 after a 2-2 draw at Anfield in 2014.

Liverpool were on the receiving end of the goal by the youngest ever goalscorer, Norman Whiteside. At the age of just 17 he scored the opener for Manchester United in the 1983 final, but The Reds equalised through Alan Kennedy before Ronnie Whelan grabbed the winner.

It was Bob Paisley's last, triumphant game as manager.

MICHAEL OWEN (2ND L) CELEBRATES WITH TEAM MATES EMILE HESKEY (L) STEPHEN GERRARD (2ND R) AND ROBBIE FOWLER (R) AFTER SCORING AGAINST ARSENAL DURING THE FA CUP FINAL AT THE MILLENNIUM STADIUM IN CARDIFF, 12 MAY 2001.

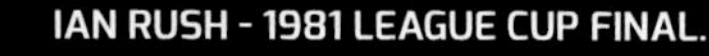

IAN RUSH - 1981 LEAGUE CUP FINAL.

RAFA BENITEZ

In Rafa we trust

RAFA BENITEZ WILL GO DOWN IN LIVERPOOL HISTORY AS THE ARCHITECT OF THE 'MIRACLE OF ISTANBUL'. ***A softly spoken Spaniard, he played for Castilla, Real Madrid's second team, but didn't progress much further as a player.*** At 26 he was given the role as coach of Real Madrid's Under 19 and reserve sides. He then had a few years learning his craft the hard way, with

Then at Valencia he won the fans over with a win over Real Madrid in his first game and took them to their first La Liga win in 31 years, and later two UEFA Cup wins.

He arrived at Liverpool in 2005 and was awarded the title of UEFA Manager of the Year for the second year running.

That award was based mainly on Liverpool's extraordinary Champions League win in Istanbul, and *Benitez is credited with the change of tactics which created that remarkable second-half turnaround.*

Another Champions League final in 2007 ended in defeat, however, with AC Milan exacting revenge for Istanbul.

Under Benitez in the 2008-09 season Liverpool came second, losing just two games. They also beat Manchester United and Chelsea home and away and Real Madrid in the Bernabeu, winning 5-0 over two legs.

Benitez left Liverpool in 2010 for Inter Milan. *At the time of writing, he is the only manager to have won the Champions League, the UEFA Cup and the FIFA Club World Cup.*

LIVERPOOL WIN THE CHAMPIONS LEAGUE FOR THE FIFTH TIME

Istanbul: the greatest night

WHETHER YOU CALL IT THE CHAMPIONS LEAGUE OR THE EUROPEAN CUP, IN 2005 LIVERPOOL CLAIMED IT FOR THE FIFTH TIME ON A CRAZY NIGHT IN ISTANBUL AND WHAT HAS COME TO BE KNOWN AS 'THE GREATEST NIGHT'.

Rafa Benitez's team had struggled in the league but had brought the electric European nights back to Anfield. Famous wins over Olympiacos, Juventus and especially Jose Mourinho's Chelsea booked The Reds' place in Istanbul.

> *"Benitez did the only two things he could – he calmed his players down and changed the system."*

Their first European Cup final appearance in 20 years, however, started badly and quickly got worse. AC Milan simply swept them aside to go in at half-time 3-0 up with goals from Paolo Maldini and Hernan Crespo (2).

Benitez did the only two things he could - he calmed his players down and changed the system. Harry Kewell had limped off in the first half and Benitez also took off Steve Finnan. *'The Kaiser' Didi Hamann* went into the centre of midfield and The Reds looked a different team.

Quick goals from a charged-up *Steven Gerrard* and Czech midfielder *Vladimir Smicer* brought Liverpool to the brink of an unlikely comeback. *Xabi Alonso* then scored from a penalty rebound to make it 3-3 and force a nervy period of extra-time.

An incredible double-save from keeper *Jerzy Dudek* kept Andriy Shevchenko from scoring, and when the Pole saved from the same player in the penalty shoot-out it was all over. Liverpool had their hands on the famous trophy yet again.

SPOTLIGHT ON:

Liverpool's tradition of great goalkeepers

LIVERPOOL HAS ALWAYS HAD A SERIOUS LOVE AFFAIR WITH GOALKEEPERS. MANY OF THE CLUB'S GREATEST PLAYERS HAVE SERVED BETWEEN THE STICKS AND THE KOP'S RESPECT FOR OPPOSITION STOPPERS IS LEGENDARY.

JERZY DUDEK

THE MEN BETWEEN THE STICKS

BRUCE GROBBELAAR

One of Liverpool's most remarkable keepers was Matt McQueen, who played mostly outfield but was happy to take the gloves when asked. In the club's very first season he filled in for original custodian William McOwen five times, and he later managed Liverpool to a title win.

There are just two other goalkeepers in the Liverpool Hall of Fame, and both can lay claim to having been

1927 - LIVERPOOL GOALKEEPER ELISHA SCOTT CLEARS THE BALL AFTER A SHOT FROM HUDDERSFIELD TOWN'S MEADS DURING THEIR MATCH UNDER WRETCHED CONDITIONS.

Belfast native ***Elisha Scott*** signed for Liverpool in 1912 and didn't leave until 1934, having played 467 games. He was not just a great servant but a superb keeper and a hugely popular figure at Anfield.

Scott would be the greatest ever by some distance were it not for a certain ***Ray Clemence.*** Another sensational shot-stopper and all-round keeper, he played 665 games all told, missing just six league matches in 11 years.

Another keeper of note included Clemence's predecessor, ***Tommy Lawrence***. Known for being both reliable and fearless, he was Bill Shankly's number one choice throughout the 60s.

Zimbabwean ***Bruce Grobbelaar*** replaced Clemence and also had a glittering career. He is fondly remembered for his wobbly-leg antics and heroic saves in the 1984 European Cup final penalty shootout.

In recent times, ***Pepe Reina*** kept a huge number of clean sheets and ***Jerzy Dudek*** was one of the heroes of Istanbul.

JAMIE CARRAGHER

The Blue who came to characterise 'The Liverpool Way'

A BORN AND BRED EVERTONIAN AND DYED IN THE WOOL SCOUSER, JAMIE CARRAGHER CAME TO EPITOMISE 'THE LIVERPOOL WAY'.

He joined the Steve Heighway-run Liverpool School of Excellence in 1990 and graduated to the first team in 1996. He made his full debut in a 3-0 win over Aston Villa, doing two things he would rarely do again for the club: scoring and playing in midfield.

'Carra' blossomed under Gerard Houllier, a manager whom he greatly respected and who played him *mainly at right-back* because of the solid centre-back partnership of Sami Hyypia and Stephane Henchoz at the time.

Few players come back stronger after breaking a leg, but that's what Carragher did. In 2004-05 Rafa Benitez moved him to the centre of the defence to partner the big Finn Hyypia and he began to play the best football of his career.

His sense of positioning, timing in the tackle and sheer energy made him possibly Liverpool's greatest ever defender.

Carragher won one European Cup, one UEFA Cup, two FA Cups, three League Cups and was capped by England 38 times.

In all he played 737 games for Liverpool, signing off in 2013. Only Ian Callaghan played more games for the club. His cramp-ignoring, socks-down performance in extra-time and then sheer jubilation during the 2005 European Cup final in Istanbul will never be forgotten.

Carragher went on to become a well-respected TV pundit on Sky, partnering one of his biggest on-field rivals, Gary Neville.

LIVERPOOL WIN THEIR SEVENTH FA CUP

The Gerrard Final

REGARDED BY MANY NEUTRALS AS THE BEST FA CUP FINAL EVER, LIVERPOOL'S VICTORY IN 2006 IS BETTER KNOWN AT THE CLUB AS THE 'GERRARD FINAL', ALTHOUGH SPANISH KEEPER PEPE REINA'S CONTRIBUTION WAS ALSO VITAL.

The road to Wembley had started at Kenilworth Road, home of Luton Town, where an end to end game saw The Reds triumph 5-3. Liverpool's goals included one from inside his own half by Xabi Alonso.

Liverpool then beat Portsmouth, Manchester United and, notably, Birmingham City 7-0 in the quarter-finals.

Similarities to the Istanbul final the previous year began to pile up when Liverpool confidently dispatched Chelsea 2-1 in the semi-final, with another goal from *Luis Garcia* being the decider.

Then in the final they found themselves drawing 3-3 after full-time and winning on penalties. And it was all down to 'Captain Fantastic' *Steven Gerrard*.

Liverpool faced a confident West Ham United in the final and were quickly 2-0 down. Gerrard, though, was having none of it. He set up *Djibril Cisse* for Liverpool's first and equalised himself after 54 minutes.

When Konchesky made it 3-2 to The Hammers, the cup looked like it was on its way to London. Again, Gerrard hadn't read the script and took the game into extra-time with a 35-yard thunderbolt, a goal as good as the final had ever seen.

Neither side could break the deadlock in extra-time but penalty kings Liverpool won out thanks to three saves from the brilliant *Reina*.

THE 2010s

LIVERPOOL'S PLAYERS CELEBRATE AFTER SCORING A GOAL DURING THEIR PREMIER LEAGUE MATCH AGAINST TOTTENHAM HOTSPUR AT WHITE HART LANE, 15 DECEMBER 2013.

AFTER A SERIOUS RIFT WITH LIVERPOOL'S AMERICAN OWNERS, GEORGE GILLETT AND TOM HICKS, RAFA BENITEZ LEFT THE CLUB IN JUNE 2010.

Benitez was replaced a month later by 63-year-old Roy Hodgson, Liverpool's first English manager since Roy Evans.

By October of the same year Gillett and Hicks had been bought out by another American group, New England Sports Ventures (now known as Fenway Sports Group), with principal owner John Henry at the helm.

Hodgson managed just 13 wins in his 31 games in charge. A home League Cup defeat to Division Two's Northampton Town, plus poor performances against Blackpool and Everton in particular, sealed his fate.

SEASON	DIVISION	P	W	D	L	F	A	D	POS
2010-11	PL	38	17	7	14	59	44	58	6th
2011-12	PL	38	14	10	14	47	40	52	8th
2012-13	PL	38	16	13	9	71	43	61	7th
2013-14	PL	38	26	6	6	101	50	84	2nd
2014-15	PL	38	18	8	12	52	48	62	6th

He left by mutual consent in January 2011 and was replaced by Reds favourite 'King' Kenny Dalglish shortly afterwards. In 2012 Dalglish led Liverpool to their eighth League Cup win as they beat Cardiff City on penalties.

The Reds were back at Wembley three months later to face Chelsea in the FA Cup final. They had started the campaign with a 5-1 win over Oldham Athletic in the third round. Strangely, they were also to face The Latics in the cup in the next two seasons, losing in the fourth round at Boundary Park in 2013 and winning 2-0 at Anfield in the third round in 2014.

In the 2012 final, Chelsea won 2-1 with goals from Ramires and Didier Drogba. *Record signing Andy Carroll grabbed The Reds' consolation.*

Unfortunately, Premier League performances were just as bad as they had been under Hodgson and by May Dalglish was gone. Liverpool struggled to eighth, four points behind Merseyside rivals Everton.

In June the club appointed young Ulsterman Brendan Rodgers as manager. He had recently brought an exciting Swansea City team into the Premier League. In his first season Liverpool improved slightly, finishing seventh but still two points behind The Toffees.

However, in 2013-14 Rodgers' team almost won the Premier League for the first time, eventually falling just short but taking champions Manchester City to the last day.

The Reds lost just one game after Christmas, had thrilled crowds across the country and had scored 101 goals.

Unfortunately, with the irreplaceable loss of Luis Suarez to Barcelona, Rodgers couldn't get his side to repeat the heroics of the previous season and he left the club in 2015.

Popular German manager Jurgen Klopp arrived soon after, and the era of 'Heavy Metal Football' had begun.

LIVERPOOL WIN THE LEAGUE CUP IN 2012

King Kenny lands yet another trophy

LIVERPOOL HAD GONE SIX YEARS WITHOUT A TROPHY WHEN KENNY DALGLISH, BACK IN HIS SECOND SPELL IN CHARGE, MANAGED TO STEER THEM TO THEIR EIGHTH LEAGUE CUP WIN.

On the journey to Wembley that season Liverpool had only played at Anfield once, in the second leg of the semi-final against Manchester City.

Wins on the road at Exeter, Brighton, Stoke and Chelsea saw them facing the new English powerhouse Manchester City at The Etihad stadium. The Reds turned in one of their best performances of the season to go back to Anfield with a precious 1-0 lead. A 2-2 home draw, with a vital late equaliser from *Craig Bellamy,* won them the tie.

The League Cup final in 2012 was the first time that *Steven Gerrard* had lined up against his cousin Anthony in a professional match, but for one of them it was to be a nightmare day.

Anthony was playing for Liverpool's opponents Cardiff City in the final of what was now known as the Carling Cup. The Reds won on penalties after a 2-2 stalemate.

The Bluebirds struck first through Joe Mason, but *Martin Skrtel* levelled after *Luis Suarez* had hit the post. Extra-time saw *Dirk Kuyt* put The Reds ahead but a Ben Turner tap-in forced penalties.

The Reds prevailed 3-2 in the shoot-out, with both Gerrards missing. Anthony's miss was Cardiff's last chance, however, and Liverpool had their *eighth League Cup* in the bag.

SPOTLIGHT ON:

The 100 per centers – the players the fans loved to love

DIRK KUYT

LIVERPOOL'S UNSUNG HEROES

LIKE ANY CLUB, LIVERPOOL HAS HAD ITS FAIR SHARE OF UNSUNG HEROES. HERE WE SALUTE THE PLAYERS THAT THE FANS LOVED TO LOVE.

Alan A'Court was the youngest Liverpool player to make 200 appearances for the club when he was just 24. He was a stalwart of Liverpool's years in the lower level wilderness in the 1950s and was *so good that he was picked for England's 1958 World Cup squad while still a Second Division player.*

So hard he was known as 'The Anfield Iron', Scouser *Tommy Smith* endeared himself to the fans with his uncompromising style. The greatest moment of his career came when his towering header put Liverpool ahead in the European Cup final in 1977.

TOMMY SMITH

Two other full-backs also make the list. First, *Joey Jones,* who also played in that game in 1977 in Rome and became the *first Welshman to win a European Cup winners' medal.* He only played 100 games for The Reds but was adored for his energy and enthusiasm.

The second full-back is *Alan Kennedy,* whose bustling style saw him christened *'Barney Rubble'* by The Kop. He replaced Jones in the team and in the fans' hearts by scoring two goals which won The Reds' European Cups in 1981 and 1984.

The most recent unsung hero, a man who always gave his all for The Reds and was loved by the fans for it, was Dutch forward *Dirk Kuyt,* scorer of many a vital goal.

ALAN KENNEDY

STEVEN GERRARD

Mr. Liverpool

'MR LIVERPOOL', STEVEN GERRARD SPENT 17 YEARS AT ANFIELD, MANY OF THEM AS CAPTAIN.

Whiston-born 'Stevie G' was quite simply one of the greatest players and inspirational leaders of his generation. He made his debut in 1998 a year after signing for the youth team.

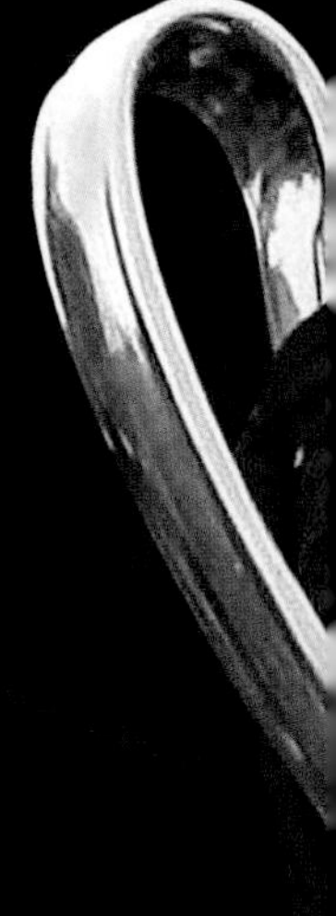

"Supremely fit, he could tackle ferociously, make slide rule passes (long and short) and shoot from anywhere."

In 2005 he was named the UEFA Club Footballer of the Year award and the winner of the Ballon d'Or Bronze Award. He was also the PFA Player's Player of the Year in 2006 and the Football Writers' Association Footballer of the year in 2009 and called 'the best player in the world' by Zinedine Zidane.

Supremely fit, he could tackle ferociously, make slide rule passes (long and short) and shoot from anywhere. His ability to grab a game by the scruff of the neck and bring Liverpool back into it was legendary.

Special goals against West Ham United in the FA Cup final and AC Milan in the Champions League final, as well as a hat-trick in the Merseyside derby in 2012, are just a few that will always be treasured by Reds fans.

Gerrard is the only player to have scored in an FA Cup final, a League Cup final, a UEFA Cup final and a Champions League final. He won two FA Cups, three League Cups, One Champions League and one UEFA Cup.

He left for LA Galaxy in 2015 having played 710 games for the club, scoring 186 times and is England's third most capped player with 114, and also scored 21 goals.

BRENDAN RODGERS AND JURGEN KLOPP

Brendan's near miss ushers in 'The Normal One'

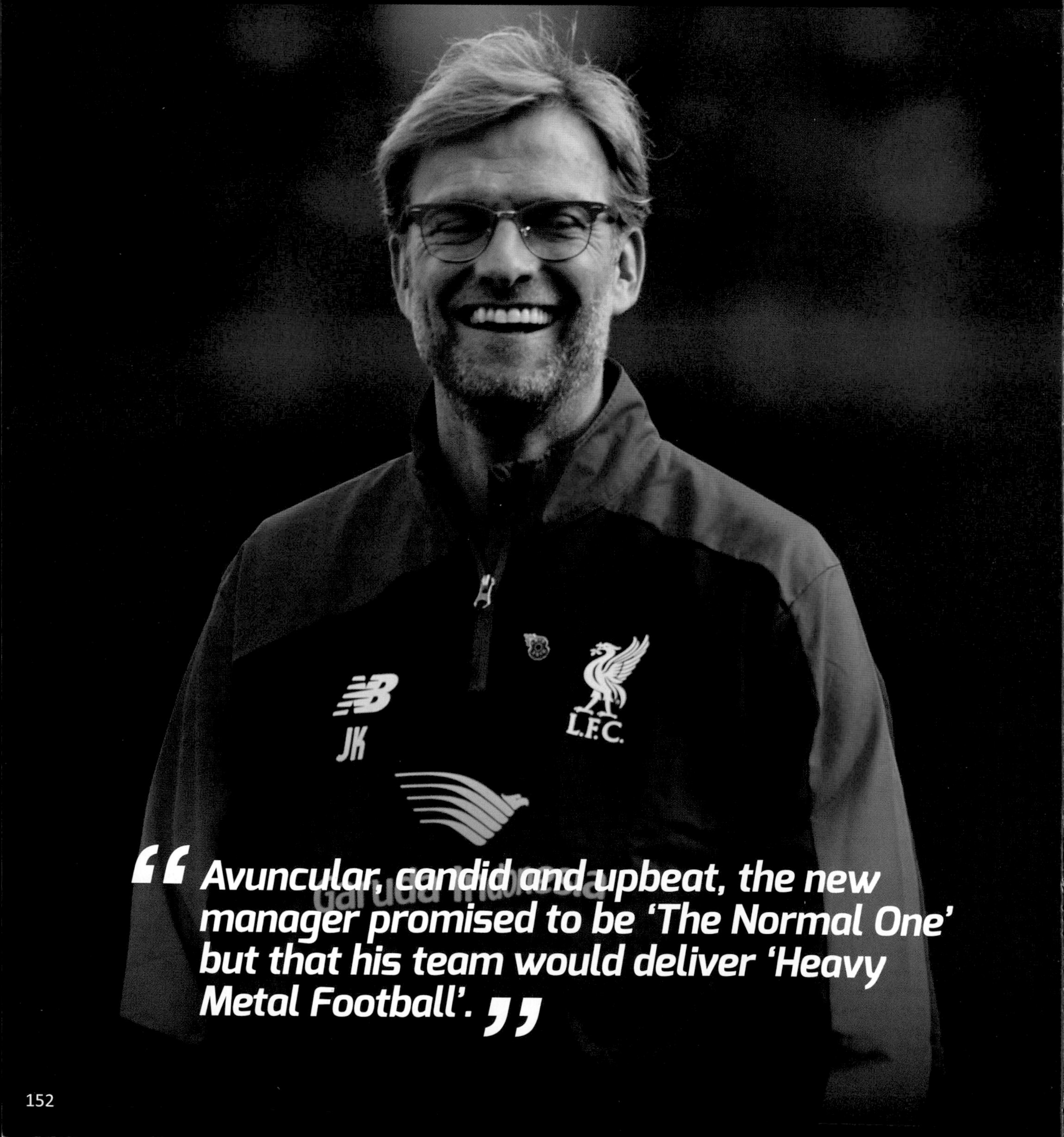

> *"Avuncular, candid and upbeat, the new manager promised to be 'The Normal One' but that his team would deliver 'Heavy Metal Football'."*

AFTER A FAILED FLIRTATION WITH ROY HODGSON AND A BRIEF RETURN FOR KENNY DALGLISH, IN 2012 LIVERPOOL APPOINTED TALENTED YOUNG ULSTERMAN BRENDAN RODGERS AS MANAGER.

He began his coaching career by managing Reading's academy, before a highly instructive spell on Jose Mourinho's staff at Chelsea.

Rodgers joined Liverpool from Swansea, whom he had skilfully guided to the Premier League in 2012.

He arrived at Anfield in June 2012 and will be remembered for getting the best out of the 'SAS' partnership of Daniel Sturridge and Luis Suarez.

A controversial figure at the best of times, Suarez was however one of the most gifted players ever to pull on the red shirt. In the 2013-14 season he netted 31 times in 33 games.

Sturridge also added 19 as Liverpool scored an incredible 101 Premier League goals.

Falling just short but taking Manchester City to the last day, Liverpool had thrilled crowds across the country and *Rodgers had made Reds fans dream again.*

Unfortunately, with the irreplaceable loss of Suarez to Barcelona, Rodgers couldn't get his side to repeat the heroics of the previous season and left the club in October 2015.

Liverpool only had one replacement in mind. German manager Jurgen Klopp had transformed Borussia Dortmund in the Bundesliga, making him much sought-after across Europe.

Avuncular, candid and upbeat, the new manager promised to be *'The Normal One'* but that his team would deliver *'Heavy Metal Football'.*

The Klopp era had begun.

LUIS SUAREZ

The Reds' unpredictable but exceptional Uruguayan

"He agreed to join Liverpool for £22.8 million, beginning another sensational and controversial chapter in his career."

BORN IN SALTO, URUGUAY, LUIS SUAREZ PLAYED JUST ONE SEASON FOR NACIONAL IN HIS HOME COUNTRY BEFORE BEING SNAPPED UP BY SCOUTS FROM GRONINGEN IN HOLLAND. HE WENT ON TO PLAY FOR AJAX, BUT AFTER BITING ANOTHER PLAYER WAS RELUCTANTLY LET GO.

He agreed to join Liverpool for £22.8 million, beginning another sensational and controversial chapter in his career.

He scored on his debut, coming on as a substitute in a 2-0 win over Stoke City, and finished the season with four goals in 13 games. However, he was banned the next season for eight matches for racially abusing Patrice Evra and ended up with just 11 goals.

In 2012-13, Suarez started to look like a world-beater. He was mercurial, with an incredible touch and specialised in amazing finishes.

He became only the third Liverpool player to score more than 20 goals in a Premier League season and finished with 30 in all competitions. But he also bit Chelsea's Branislav Ivanovic and was banned again, this time for ten games.

He returned to The Reds side in September 2013 and by the end of that season had smashed all kinds of records, *scoring 31 goals in just 33 games,* most of them world-class. He won the Premier League Golden Boot, the Player of the Year award and shared the European Golden Shoe with Cristiano Ronaldo.

He signed for Barcelona in 2014, having netted 82 goals in 133 games for The Reds, but still had time to bite his third player, Giorgio Chiellini of Italy, at the World Cup in Brazil.

SPOTLIGHT ON:

22 of the club's greatest ever players

ALBERT STUBBINS

LIVERPOOL'S HALL OF FAME WAS INAUGURATED IN 2002. IT WAS CREATED AFTER WEEKS OF DISCUSSION AND CONSULTATION WITH SUPPORTERS GROUPS BY TWO EVENTUAL INDUCTEES, IAN CALLAGHAN AND ALAN HANSEN. THEY WERE HELPED BY FORMER SKIPPER PHIL THOMPSON AND SHANKLY FAVOURITE BRIAN HALL.

Two players were chosen from each decade of the last century to make the list of just 22 players. Callaghan and company certainly had some tough choices to make, and there's no d[illegible]bt Reds fans will always argue f[illegible] the i[illegible]usion of their particular favourites.

LIVERPOOL'S HALL OF FAME

As for the next players to make the cut, the club's website says "A further two (players) will be added shortly to represent the first decade of the new millennium".

By decade, the current Liverpool Football Club Hall of Fame is:

1890s
Harry Bradshaw, Striker, 1893-1898
Matt McQueen, Goalkeeper, 1892-1899

1900s
Jack Cox, Left Midfield, 1897-1909
Alex Raisbeck, Central Defender, 1898-1909

1910s
Arthur Goddard, Right Midfield, 1902-1914
Elisha Scott, Goalkeeper, 1912-1934

1920s
Donald MacKinlay, Right Back, 1910-1929
Ephraim Longworth, Right Back, 1910-1928

1930s
Jimmy McDougall, Central Defender, 1928-1938
Gordon Hodgson, Striker, 1925-1936

ALAN HANSEN

KENNY DALGLISH

1940s
Jack Balmer, Striker, 1935-1952
Albert Stubbins, 1946-1953

1950s
Alan A'Court, Left Midfield, 1952-1964
Billy Liddell, 1939-1961

1960s
Roger Hunt, Striker, 1958-1969
Ron Yeats, Central Defender, 1961-1971

1970s
Ian Callaghan, Right Midfield, 1960-1978
Ray Clemence, Goalkeeper, 1967-1981

1980s
Kenny Dalglish, Striker, 1977-1991
Alan Hansen, Central Defender, 1977-1991

1990s
Ian Rush, Striker, 1980-1996
John Barnes, Left Midfield, 1987-1997

THE TROPHY CABINET

Liverpool's complete list of honours

LIVERPOOL'S HEAVING TROPHY CABINET HAS TO BE SEEN TO BE BELIEVED. IT ALL STARTED IN THE VERY FIRST SEASON IN 1892-93 WHEN THEY WON THE LANCASHIRE LEAGUE.

The club have now won more European trophies than any other team in England and have won 18 League championships.

The players have ***29 individual honours*** between them in the 41 years since Ian Callaghan picked up the Football Writers' Association Footballer of the Year Award in 1974.

The full list of senior honours (as at 2015) is:

18 First Division Championships
7 FA Cups
8 League Cups*
5 European Cups*
3 UEFA Cups*
3 European Super Cups
15 Charity Shields (5 shared)
1 Screen Sport Super Cup
***English club record**

In addition, ***The Reds have won four Second Division titles*** and ***won the old reserves title, the Central League, 16 times.*** The youth team won the FA Youth Cup three times.

Individual player awards include:

1 European Footballer of the Year (Michael Owen) in 2001
12 Football Writers' Association Footballer of the Year Awards
6 PFA Player of the Year Awards
5 PFA Young Player of the Year Awards
3 PFA Fans' Player of the Year Awards
2 European Golden Boot Awards

Liverpool managers have also won the Manager of the Year Award 11 times.

THIS IS
LIVER POOL
FOOTBALL CLUB
ANFIELD